D1003759

A decade has passed since the first printing of Ocean City: A Pictorial History. Its popularity has been a gratifying experience for both the authors and the townspeople. The Board of Directors of the Ocean City Museum Society are proud to sponsor the third printing of the book. By doing so, the society is commemorating the 100th anniversary of the building of the present United States Life-Saving Station Museum, the historic showplace of our community.

Ocean City

A PICTORIAL HISTORY

BY
GEORGE M. HURLEY
SUZANNE B. HURLEY

Design by
Fischbach & Edenton

DONNING COMPANY/PUBLISHERS
VIRGINIA BEACH, VIRGINIA

Looking north from First Street, 1894.
Courtesy of Ocean City
Museum Society.

The Ocean City Coast Guard march as a unit in the annual Fireman's Parade during 1929. Courtesy of Mary "Boots" Mason

Copyright © 1979 by George and Suzanne Hurley
Revised third printing, 1991
All rights reserved, including the right to reproduce this book in any form whatsoever without permission in writing from the publisher, except for brief passages in connection with a review. For information, write:

The Donning Company/Publishers
184 Business Park Drive, Suite 106
Virginia Beach, Virginia 23462

Library of Congress Cataloging in Publication Data:

1.   Ocean City, Md.--History--Pictorial works.
2.   Ocean City, Md.--Description--Views. I. Hurley, Suzanne; joint author.
II. Title.
F189.02H87   975.2'21   79-15873
ISBN 0-915442-98-1
ISBN 0-89865-002-X deluxe

Printed in the United States of America

In this early 1940s boardwalk scene the beach has begun to widen through the use of jetties placed there in the mid-teens.
Courtesy of Ocean City Public Relations

TO OUR CHILDREN
JEFFERY, DAPHNE, MARK & ERIC

Preface

The graphic materials included in this collection represent segments of the history of Ocean City. It is not a complete story, but does represent a studious effort to collect and place under one cover materials that early residents felt worthy of photographing and saving through the years. The contents have come from family albums, musty attics, and literally off the walls of homes. Contemporary photographs were found in local newspaper files and private collections. We have relied heavily on the memories of older members of the community who made themselves available.

Pictures of individuals have been included only as participants in the events of this history. It is to be regretted that more pictures were not available for inclusion.

Events have been chronologically presented along with unique photographs which depict our early and contempory lifestyle. Ocean City has moved through a transition from a small fishing village to a major coastal resort in the past one hundred years. If this book has captured a part of that change, then it has served its purpose.

We are grateful to Thelma Connor for introducing us to Monty Joynes of the Donning Company/Publishers and for encouraging the publication of this book.

William D. Pitts, George B. Cropper, Norman K. Jones, William H. Purnell, Jr., William H. Purnell, Sr., and Daniel Prettyman provided valuable information and documents concerning the founding of Ocean City.

A special thank you to Donna Reiss Friedman for her expertise in editing this book; also to Larry Bright and Holly Bounds for carefully handling and reproducing the photographs; and to Dale and Suzanne Timmons for patiently proofreading the captions.

Most helpful were Paul Guite of the National Archives, Washington, D.C., and Kent Griffith of the Ocean City Museum Society.

We are extremely grateful to the individuals whose names appear with the captions under each photograph. This book would not have been possible without the generosity of Mrs. Joshua Bunting, Kathryn Jones Bunting, Thelma Dennis, Mr. and Mrs. William Matthews, Annie Quillen, Melville Quillin, Violet C. Davis, Elizabeth Gordy, the Ocean City Public Relations Department, and the Eastern Shore Times, Inc., who made their large photographic collections available.

Many pleasurable hours were spent reminiscing and critiquing this collection with Alan Quillin, Ellen Weaver, Daniel Trimper III, Mr. and Mrs. W. Preston Laws, Mr. and Mrs. J.D. Quillin III, Annie Bunting, and Mr. and Mrs. William P. Burbage.

A special thank you is extended to our children for their patience and understanding.

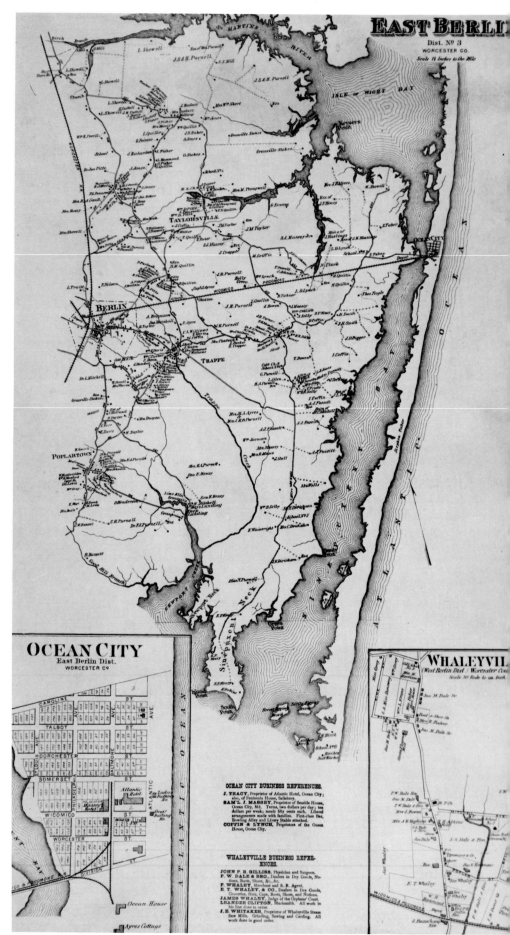

This 1877 map of East Berlin, Worcester County, Maryland, in which Ocean City is first shown, shows an approximate ten mile proximity of the resort. On the large map can be found the names of many of the town's founders and early investors. An insert to the left shows that during this period less than fifteen buildings existed on the island.

Courtesy of John E. Jacob, Jr., for the Wicomico Bicentennial Commission

Introduction

Early in this century, a character in John Dos Passos' novel *The 42nd Parallel* spent the summer at the Ocean House and wrote: "the life giving surges of the broad Atlantic beat on the crystalline beaches of Ocean City, Maryland...the tonic breath of the pines brings relief to the asthmatic and the consumptive." There can be little doubt that the great natural beauty of the geographical setting, with its clean air, unlimited expanses of salt water, and clean, white sandy beaches, has been the primary attraction of Ocean City.

The saga of the city's history and development is an exciting and phenomenal success story. Nurtured from the imaginations of a handful of enterprising businessmen seeking to establish a seaside resort after the great Civil War, Ocean City has grown from two small cottages into what is generally regarded as Maryland's second largest city during the traditional summer vacation months.

Ocean City is virtually an island, geologically defined as a barrier beach. It is bordered on the west by the Sinepuxent, Isle of Wight, and Assawoman Bays. On the east, the Atlantic Ocean washes its sandy shores, while to the north it blends into the coastal expanses of Delaware. Until the 1933 storm created an inlet to the south, it was a continuation of Assateague Island, which was so named by the gentle Indian tribe of the same name found in the area by the earliest settlers and meaning "place across."

In the earliest times, Pocomoke, Chincoteague, and Assateague Indians of the Nanticoke tribe lived in the general area adjacent to Ocean City, evidenced by the many artifacts that have been found through the years in West Ocean City, including a large burial area on the high knoll that used to exist near the entrance of the first state highway bridge into the resort. These people were probably the first to realize the beauty and richness of the area for sustenance. It is a matter of record that the first contact in 1649 with the Assateagues indicated a peaceful and gentle tribe who guided shipwrecked and lost colonists back to the Virginia settlement, while graciously sharing their food and belongings.

Continuing encroachment on the part of the English colonists resulted in the creation of a reservation named Askiminokonson near present-day Snow Hill, Maryland, to which many of the subtribes migrated, including the Assateagues. It was the largest Indian town in Maryland by 1671. Fearful of their future in the area, the group began migrating northward in 1748. Historians trace their route of assimilation and integration with other tribes through their language as they moved northward through Pennsylvania and New York to Canada, where they were lost to history.

One of the earliest European references to this section of Assateague Island was made by the explorer Giovanni da Verrazano, who was sailing under the French flag. Observing it in 1524, he described it as very lush and beautiful, and named it Arcadia. Today, a bridge extending to the government-controlled portion of the island is named in his honor. The island is not

Congress Hall Hotel as it appeared in 1881.
Courtesy of
Mr. and Mrs. Anthony Purnell

The Baltimore, Chesapeake and Atlantic Railway published prior to 1896 this artist's conception entitled "Sinepuxent Beach, Ocean City, Maryland." Starting with the second building from the left of the photograph are: Cambridge Hotel, Congress Hall, Seabright Hotel, E. Hobbs Bath House connecting with the Eastern Shore Hotel, Hotel DeCropper, Hotel Belvedere, Casino, Cottage, Atlantic Hotel and dancing pavilion, Ladies Bath, cottage, cottage, cottage, Isle of Wight Hotel, cottage, cottage, and the Life-Saving Station. The Seaside Hotel is in the center of town on Baltimore Avenue.
Courtesy of Larry Bright

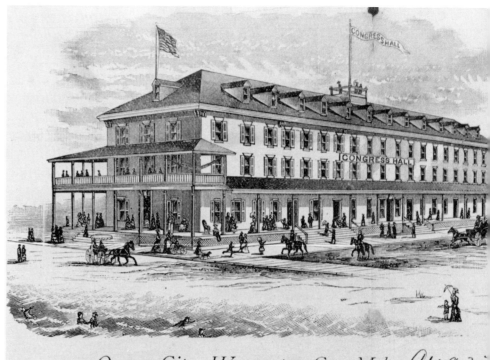

Ocean City, Worcester Co., Md. Aug 2

Ocean City's first mayor was William Sidney Wilson. The son of United States Senator Ephriam King Wilson, he was born and lived near Snow Hill, Maryland. In 1877 Wilson was elected to the House of Delegates, and in 1883 he was elected state's attorney of Worcester County. He also was quite successful in fields other than law; he was a prominent banker and investor, was well-traveled, and was noted for his engaging social qualities; he was on the board of directors of the Sinepuxent Beach Corporation and was instrumental in the development of Ocean City, serving as mayor from 1892 to 1896. Wilson ended his own life at the age of forty-five. This photograph was taken from an old, undated newspaper clipping found in an attic in Ocean City. Courtesy of Ocean City Museum Society

without its legends; stories abound regarding famous pirates and the treasures they supposedly buried in the area. Much time and money have been expended looking for such depositories, since some of the stories have been reasonably authenticated. Little is known, however, regarding any successful ventures.

Although settlements existed on Assateague Island during the early nineteenth century, the nearest such village to Ocean City would have been North Beach, approximately ten miles to the south. A probable explanation for the absence of early development where Ocean City exists today could be geographical. Most settlements relied upon agricultural products and in addition needed grazing land for livestock. This section of Assateague Island was very narrow when compared to the southern areas of the island and could not offer the high ground required for gardens and livestock.

Politically, all of Assateague Island and the lands northward to Cape Henlopen once belonged to Lord Baltimore, proprietor of Maryland, by royal decree of the King of England. In fact, according to *Worcester County: Maryland's Arcadia*, fifty acres of land was once set aside by Lord Baltimore's authority on Indian River in present-day Delaware, to create the city of Baltimore. In various ways, Lord Baltimore's family lost control of a large part of their land holdings. Today, the boundaries of Worcester County, Maryland's easternmost county, begin twenty miles to the south of the Ocean City inlet on Assateague Island and terminate in the north of Ocean City at the east-west extension of the famous Mason-Dixon Line. (Mason and Dixon did not survey this particular line, however.) Governmental agencies own and control Assateague Island today, while Ocean City has been developed by private enterprise on the northward part of what once was Assateague and Fenwick Island.

The most important role in the successful growth of Ocean City has been played by its people. Regrettably, it is impossible to identify all of the many people who have shared in the city's development through its formative years. Suffice it to say that the elegance and luxuriousness associated with the city today evolved from more austere settings. Earlier generations were geographically isolated in Worcester County; this caused the culture to develop with a leisurely pace and life-style. The land and waters of this section of the Eastern Shore of Maryland contributed greatly to the serenity, making fine sustenance available through a bountiful supply of agricultural products, seafood, and wild fowl, with few people harvesting it. This richness could possibly explain the easy-going character of the residents and, more importantly, the leisure time to enjoy it, resulting in "the good life." To be sure, working the land and sea were difficult, which some say is good for a person's character; but the slow pace and ease of living created a personality most regard as very sociable, but plainspoken, with a touch of salt.

Ocean City has always enjoyed a reputation for genuine hospitality that came naturally with the earliest families who hosted guests at the turn of the century; this graciousness matured with their children and with the many new residents who came each year and decided to call Ocean City home. Of no little significance in this regard have been Ocean City women, who have traditionally played key roles in the creation of the industry that is today the economic backbone of the area, namely the hospitality industry. It is interesting to note, in fact, that long before the village was laid out, the owner of the land, Mr. Stephen Taber, had dubbed this parcel "Ladies Resort to the Ocean."

Traditionally, according to Robbins and Henley, credit is given to Isaac Coffin for building in the area of Ocean City the first beachfront cottage that hosted paying guests. This was in 1869, and his guests would come by stagecoach or wagon and then be ferried to the island by a small boat. Guests were primarily fishermen who cast along the surf bank. The occasional family that accompanied the fishermen either fished also, or strolled along the beach. Coffin named his small guest home the Rhode Island Inn, reportedly from a ship's signboard that had floated ashore at about that time. Several prominent families today can indirectly trace their ancestry to Isaac Coffin, and many are still professionally involved in entertaining paying guests, though on a much more sophisticated level.

Coffin was followed by James Massey of Berlin, Maryland. Massey constructed a boarding house for guests near Coffin's cottage in 1872. The exact location of both buildings is uncertain, since various accounts recall facts differently. Most sources place Coffin's venture somewhere in the area of the present-day inlet or just a little to the south of it. It is a fact that Ocean House, owned by Coffin and Lynch, is shown on an 1877 insurance map between South Second Street and Third Street. This is, of course, the present-day inlet. The Massey dwelling was supposedly near Coffin's, but most accounts acknowledge that it was located at the intersection of Wicomico Street and Baltimore Avenue, and was

A rare find was this share of stock in the Wicomico and Pocomoke Rail Road Company, whose major stockholders were also those who had invested heavily in the development of Ocean City. There is some doubt that the town would have progressed without this rail line, for access to the island was a prime growth factor.

Courtesy of Thelma Dennis and family

The famous Atlantic Hotel as it appeared in 1921. Built in 1875 by the Atlantic Hotel Corporation, it was considered Ocean City's grandest hotel. An early 1891 advertisement states, "The Atlantic Hotel and Casino affords an endless round of popular and pleasant amusements. The pavilion for dancing, etc., is the finest on the Peninsula. A first-class orchestra will furnish music throughout the season. A billiard and pool room, including a handsome buffet, is attached to the house." This building burned in 1925, and was replaced by a larger, more modern building of the same name. The hotel is today owned and operated by the William H. Purnell family.

Courtesy of Maryland Historical Trust, Margaret Carey Collection

Members of the Ayres family on the beach in 1901. Left to right; Guy R. Ayres, Mary Ayres, unknown, Margarette Ayres, Samuel J. Ayres, Aralanta Ayres, unknown.

Courtesy of Michael Day from the collection of Virginia Ayres Satterfield

A view of the Seabright Hotel, Congress Hall, and various cottages located at the south end of the resort before the turn of the century.
Courtesy of Mr. and Mrs. William Matthews and family

added onto later to become the Seaside Hotel.

In the year 1868 an organization known as the Atlantic Hotel Company Corporation, with Hillary R. Pitts as president and B. Jones Taylor as treasurer, was formed. It was the desire of the members of this corporation to create a seaside resort.

During July of 1872, the same year that Massey was building, the *Salisbury Advertiser* reported that a prominent group of Eastern Shore, Baltimore, and Philadelphia businessmen visited the beach to select a site for development. Some of the names became prominent in the actual start of development: Lemuel Showell, R. Jenkins Henry, Dr. Hammond, George W. Purnell, and B. Jones Taylor of the Berlin area; Purnell Toadvine of Salisbury; Emily Jones of Princess Anne; Colonel and Mrs. Levin Woolford, Dr. William H. Gale, Levin L. Waters and son Alonza, F. E. Ziegler, and Frank Fowler of Baltimore; and John E. Husband of Philadelphia. The group visited the island on a July afternoon and selected a site of approximately ten acres across from the hammocks, or narrowest part of Sinepuxent Bay, which they planned to develop. The Atlantic Hotel Company Corporation officers approached the wealthy Long Island, New York, man who owned the property under consideration. His name was Stephen Taber, and he had only recently acquired the property (with a partner, who was later bought out) through a patent from the state of Maryland in 1868. Taber and his wife Rosetta listened with interest to the proposition made by the business group, whereby they felt there was a genuine desire on the part of the people of the county to have a seaside retreat established in the area. It must be speculated that Taber consented verbally to their wishes by letting them select ten acres upon which they were to build a hotel, within a fifty-acre parcel he would consider granting as a site for a possible town. He did not at this time deed any property to the group. There is some reason to believe, however, that he might have become a shareholder in the corporation.

The group sold four thousand shares of stock with a par value of twenty-five dollars each. After raising the one hundred thousand dollars needed, they proceeded to have the community surveyed and subdivided into 205 building lots, including north-south avenues and east-west streets. Daniel Calib Hudson was the surveyor. Beginning with a Division Street in the south, the east-west streets were named after the counties of the Eastern Shore of Maryland: Worcester, Wicomico, Somerset, Dorchester, Talbot, and Caroline. In the original Hudson plat there was no North Division Street. The north-south avenues from ocean to bay were named respectively: Atlantic (boardwalk), Baltimore, Philadelphia, and St. Louis.

While this organizational work was proceeding, the group was forming plans for an extension of the Wicomico and Pocomoke Rail Road line from Berlin, Maryland, to the new development. Hillary R. Pitts was also president of that corporation; later Lemuel Showell would head it. R. Jenkins Henry was treasurer. The rail route was extended to the mainland side of the Sinepuxent Bay in 1874. During 1874, construction

Margaret Campbell Buell, the daughter of Frank L. Campbell, the assistant secretary of the Interior, and assistant attorney general of the U.S. for the Interior Department, and wife of Willard E. Buell, chief in the Treasury Department. Mrs. Buell built the Mount Pleasant Hotel in 1900. Many prominent government officials vacationed at her hotel. After many years in business, Mrs. Buell sold the hotel and retired to St. Augustine, Florida, where she died in 1943.

15

ALPHABETICAL LIST OF ORIGINAL INVESTORS IN LOTS PLATTED BY THE ATLANTIC HOTEL CORPORATON BETWEEN SOUTH DIVISION STREET AND CAROLINE STREET IN OCEAN CITY, MARYLAND.
(AUGUST 31, 1875)

ABEL, A.S.
ATLANTIC HOTEL CORP.
BAKER, ROBERT
BALES, JOSEPH W. JR.
BARNUMS HOTEL
BELLAH,?
BIRLHEAD, WILLIAM
BOSS, JAMES
BUNTING-DUNBOROW CO.
CAREY, ELIJAH
COFFIN, C.E.
COLB, E.R.E.
DALE, JOHN M. SR.
DASHIELL, L.L. & CO.
DAVIS, PETER L.
DENNIS, GEORGE R.
DENNIS, JAMES
DENNIS, S.P.
DERIEKSON, JAMES B.
DIRICKSON, JAMES C.
DOUGHER, C.G.
ELLIOTT, ?
FASSITT, E.F.
FASSITT, HOMER
FOOKS, RITCHIE
FOWLER, J.H.
FRANKLIN, L.P.
GALLAGER, CHARLES J.
GANTZ, H.
GANTZ, T.S.
GOLDSBOROUGH, GEORGE R.
GRAHMAN, S.A.
GRINDALL, JOSEPH
GUMBY, L.W.
HARRISON BROS. & CO.

HANTILGE, ?
HASTINGS, S.M.
HAMBLIN, JOHN
HAMILTON, W.T.
HENRY, Z.P.
HERMAN, G.N.
HERSAM, WILLIAM
HIGGINS, E. JR.
HUMPHREYS, THOMAS
HURLEY, W.H.
HOOPER, W.H. DR.
JACKSON, E.E. CO.
JOHNSON, W.T.
JONES, I.S.
JONES, MARGARET
LAWSON, R.
LEA? SON, WILLIAM
LYNCH, L.D.
MALONE, LEM
MANNERS FISH & OYSTER CO.
MASSEY & CO.
MASSEY, JAMES
MELSON, L.S. & BROS.
MEYERS, JOHN B.
MULLEN, G.W.
MYERS, NATHON
NELSON, C.P.
PARSONS, A.F.
PARSONS, GEORGE H.
PITTS, H.R.
POLLS, H.N.
PURNELL, GEORGE W.
PURNELL, JOHN R.
PURNELL, JOHN S.
PURNELL, NANCY

PHEOBUS,?
RABLSON & DIXON
RIDE, THOMAS F.J.
RIDER,?
ROCKHILL, JOHN C.
ROSP, JOHN
SAMUEL, EDWARD
SAMUEL, JOSEPH LEE
SCISSORS, HUGH
SELBY, H.C.
SELBY, WILLIAM B.R.
SHOWELL, LEMUEL
SHOWELL, WILLIAM
STELL, MATHEW T.
STEWART, JAMES A.
STOKES, P.
TABER, STEPHEN
TAYLOR, B. JONES
TAYLOR, JOHN M.
THOMAS, P.S.
TOADVINE, E.S.
TRACY, JOHN
ULMAN, S.
WATERS, L.
WALLER, E.C.
WICOMICO & POCOMOKE RAILROAD
WELLS, C., MRS.
WHALEY, JAMES
WHALEY, T.
WHALEY, S.M.
WHALEY, THOMAS
WILLIAMS, C.L.
WILSON, E.K.
WOLLARD, LEVIN
WORKMAN, H.W.

A scene of the train on the trestle bridge approaching Ocean City during the 1890s. This picture was taken looking toward West Ocean City, showing the bridge draw behind the train. This was the only bridge across the Sinepuxent Bay to the beach from 1876 until 1916. A toll of five cents was collected from pedestrians and vehicular traffic using the often-swaying span.
Courtesy of Mr. and Mrs. William Matthews and family

A builder's photograph of the Wicomico and Pocomoke Rail Road engine *L. Showell* in March 1868. Lemuel Showell was one of the road's major backers and later its president. The Wicomico and Pocomoke began operations between Berlin and Salisbury, Maryland, in May of 1868. The line was extended to Sinepuxent Bay by September 1874 and later across the bay to the beach.
Courtesy of H. L. Broadbelt; collection of Kent Griffith

work commenced on the original Atlantic Hotel, which was ready for occupancy and dedication on July 4, 1875. A reporter for the *Salisbury Advertiser* wrote of the occasion:

On Monday, 5th inst., we took the cars (railroad) at this place [Salisbury] at 6 o'clock, in company with several hundred others, en route for the new seaside resort known as Ocean City, in Worcester County, Maryland, arriving at the new Atlantic Hotel about 8 o'clock, where we found a large number of guests who were glad to see us, or seemed so at least. [The train went only to West Ocean City, and boats were used to get to the island.] During the day, numerous other arrivals took place. A large number of sailing yachts, a steamship, and three other trains, one from Lewis, one from Snow Hill, and another from Salisbury, which altogether brought to Ocean City about eight hundred persons, including the visitors who had arrived in advance of us. The hotel is a marvel in architectural beauty and excellence rivaling the finest hotel on the Atlantic Coast. The rooms are large and airy with the best ventilation we ever saw.

The stockholders had held a meeting in Salisbury and named the venture. Sinepuxent City and Beach City were considered, but, as the reporter noted above, Ocean City proved to be the most popular. The original Hudson plat, dated August 31, 1875, shows that 104 different individuals agreed to purchase the first lots in the subdivision. According to some sources, original deeds show that these first lots were the result of drawings from a jar, afforded only to shareholders in the Atlantic Hotel Company Corporation. In either case the development (though not a corporation) had acquired a name, a major hotel, and at least 104 lot owners by that date. A year later, on July 28, 1876, Stephen Taber fully deeded over "Ocean City, Maryland," with the Atlantic Hotel Company Corporation officers, B. Jones Taylor, George W. Purnell, and Hillary R. Pitts as trustees. A graphic copy of an early plat is included in this history, while a full size copy of the original plat is on display in the Ocean City Life-Saving Station Museum.

It has been reported that many hearty laughs were directed towards the group for so foolhardy an undertaking, with detractors claiming that no building would be able to withstand the northwesterly winds on the island. Others contended that people with good sense would not consider living or vacationing in such an isolated and desolate spot. Although some accounts contend that the hotel had a difficult time during that first year, it is interesting to note that James Massey enlarged his cottage into the much larger Seaside Hotel the following year, suggesting successful acceptance by the public.

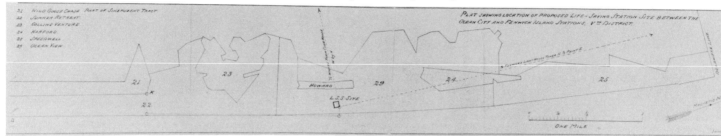

This 1897 plat of North Ocean City shows Thirty-Third Street to the Delaware line. The Life-Saving Station site marked on the plat was located at today's Eighty-Fifth Street.

Courtesy of National Archives

By 1876 the railroad had extended the track across the bay on a trestle type bridge that entered the resort at about present-day South Division Street and turned north up Baltimore Avenue to a depot in front of the Seaside Hotel. Later the station was moved behind the Seaside Hotel to Philadelphia Avenue between Wicomico and Somerset streets, where the bricks of its platform are still evident today and are used as a city sidewalk. The first wood-burning locomotive had come to Ocean City in 1874 as far as the bay. In 1893 Edward S. Furbush of Berlin drove the first coal-burning locomotive into Ocean City. In his novel *Lost in the Funhouse*, John Barth recounted such an experience:

> Thrice a year, on Memorial, Independence, and Labor days the family visits Ocean City for the afternoon and evening. When Ambrose and Peter's father was their age, the excursion was made by train. Many families from the same neighborhood used to travel together, with dependent relatives and often negro servants; schoolfuls of children swarmed through the railroad cars; everyone shared everyone else's Maryland fried chicken, Virginia ham, deviled eggs, potato salad, beaten biscuits, iced tea.

The railroad was a significant factor in public acceptance of Ocean City. Although there had been many prior attempts to establish small seaside resort developments on Assateague Island, some of which had been moderately successful, the presence of the railroad attracted increasing numbers of residents and guests to Ocean City. Employment with the railroad provided a prestigious and secure year-round income, and the families of railroad workers found Ocean City living to be attractive. The railroad era and the people directly related to it proved very valuable to the community, producing leaders in politics, civil services, education, and skilled crafts.

The pound fishing industry, summer tourism, and the Life-Saving Station increased the population and the stability of the fledgling town. In 1878, just three years after the dedication of the

Atlantic Hotel, the federal government established a Life-Saving Station on the northern edge of the village (Caroline Street); it was one of a series of such installations along the east coast during the era of great sailing ships and heavy post-Civil War coastal shipping. The station became an integral part of the fabric of the community over the years, and its personnel established a record of assistance to seamen and to the community unsurpassed along the coast. They were, in fact, during the early years of the history of the village, a combination of Coast Guard, Volunteer Fire Department, and Beach Patrol (lifeguards), before any of these organizations existed here. Many prominent community leaders, including at least two mayors, came from the ranks of life-saving personnel stationed locally. The following anecdote supplied by the National Archives from the *Annual Report, U. S. Life-Saving Service*, 1883, exemplifies rescues made by the Ocean City Life-Saving Station and depicts the difficult conditions under which they worked:

On January 10, 1883, another wreck, involving loss of life, took place on the coast of the fifth district, in the height of a storm (of violent nature). The vessel concerned was the three-masted schooner *Sallie W. Kay*, of Somers Point, N. J., bound from Baltimore to Boston, with a cargo of coal, and having a crew of seven men. Sailing in the heart of the chaos of snow, she suddenly brought up hard and fast aground. The moment she struck, the watch below rushed up on deck, and all hands made haste to lower the yawl. Before it could be done, it was swept away. The next moment the crew had to fly aloft into the rigging. Sea after sea came charging over the stern, scattering and staving in all directions. Before long water poured in, filling and sinking the schooner. Fearing that the masts would fall, they clambered out on to the jib boom and protected themselves by wrapping the jib sail around themselves.

James Zeno Powell, a prominent Worcester County businessman, was affiliated with both the Atlantic and Congress Hall Hotels. He served as mayor of the town form 1898 to 1899.

Courtesy of James Z. Powell family

Isle of Wight Life-Saving Station, shown in 1910, was built in 1897 on a barren stretch of beach located between Ocean City and Fenwick, Delaware: this dangerous section of beach was not easily accessible either to Ocean City or Fenwick crews in case of a shipwreck. The station was constructed at approximately today's Eighty–Fifth Street. Decommissioned in 1935, it went through a series of private ownerships, was badly damaged by the Storm of 1962, and was subsequently burned to the ground by request of the owners.

Though the men who manned this station saw little activity through the years, there came ashore on the night of November 25, 1900, the British steamer *Margaret Jones*. Bound from Malta to the Delaware Breakwater light, she grounded just two hundred yards south of the station. She carried a crew of twenty-two, who refused to abandon ship. The men of Isle of Wight station spent five days assisting the wrecking tug *North America* in refloating the vessel.

Courtesy of Ocean City Museum
Society, the Ella B. Quillin collection

Personnel of the Life-Saving Station at Ocean City pose at the turn of the century. The equipment pictured here had a total weight of 1,500 pounds and was pulled by these men over sandy and often badly flooded beach. In the 1883 rescue of the *Sallie W. Kay*, this cart was pulled for ninety-six city blocks, through a blinding snowstorm.

Courtesy of Kathryn Jones Bunting

The schooner had struck upon a bar some five and a half miles north of the Ocean City, Md. Station (W. T. West, Keeper). [This would be approximately in the area of the present-day Golden Sands building.] It was an hour before the snow allowed them a glimpse of the beach and a solitary dwelling to the northwest. The house belonged to a fisherman named Howard and a son of his saw the wreck and called his father. The high storm tide was running across the beach to the bay beyond, so that to notify the men at the station was impracticable. When the tide began to fall, the boy was dispatched for the station.

The sailors were maintaining their weary watch upon the jib when one of them, a young and powerful German named Anton, declared he was going to swim ashore for assistance. For a long time, his comrades watched him, and saw him again and again nearly affect a landing, but he was borne back at each approach by the powerful undertow. At last he was swept away to the south still battling.

The patrolman who had started out from the station in the morning, after an exhausting trudge of a couple of hours, was unable to make more than a mile and a half and was forced to retreat to the station, arriving at 8 o'clock. His way had been through blinding snow and spray, which rendered vision impossible. The beach was trenched with gullies and in low places he was hip deep. Where the water did not reach there was snow twenty inches deep and up to the waist in drifts.

A rare photograph of the actual construction of the pier, dated 1904. In July of 1907, the *Salisbury Advertiser* heralded the completion of the pier saying, "It is one of the greatest improvements Ocean City has made." Built by the Ocean City Pier Improvement Company, with William Taylor as president, the new attraction housed a dancing pavilion, skating rink, bowling alleys, pool room, theatre, and refreshment booths. The building, bearing little resemblance to the original, remains today a popular tourist attraction.

Courtesy of Mr. and Mrs. William Matthews and family

The Talbot Inn on the corner of Baltimore Avenue and Talbot Street as it appeared in 1920. The sign advertised meals, room and board. To the best of our knowledge the inn-home was built by William Taylor around 1903.

Courtesy of Mary Mason

A rare view of the Plimhimmon Hotel, taken in 1901. The owner of this hotel, Rosalie Tilghman Shreve, a widow with children to support, came to the village during the summer months and ran the Goldsborough cottage. Finding this venture successful and prosperous, she built in 1894 the Plimhimmon. Regretfully, we have no photograph of Mrs. Shreve, for she and her family played an important role in the development of the hospitality industry in Ocean City.
Courtesy of Mr. and Mrs. William Matthews and family

During a lull, one of the station crew from the lookout platform atop the building caught sight of the distant schooner. Keeper West at once ordered out the apparatus, but realizing the impossibility of pulling it with men (as was normal), he dispatched a man for a pair of oxen.

The journey north was terrible. The men buckled to with the oxen, tugging the loaded mortar cart, with its thousand pounds of weight over the snow-clogged, torn and flooded beach, and against the onset of the gale. Midway they met the little messenger toiling towards them, and at a quarter past two, arrived in front of the vessel.

The men were exhausted and paused a few moments to recover. It was a little space, however, before the mortar cart was unloaded and the gun trained. At the first shot the line flew over the foretopmast stay, and the bight slipped down within reach of the sailors, who at once began to haul in. They were so numbed and cramped with their long confinement upon the spar, beaten by the cold gale and snow, that it was with some difficulty they could gather in the whip line. But before long the lines were set up and the breeches buoy rigged on, and in half an hour the six men were landed safely. The sailors were in an almost dying condition upon landing, and were helped down the long beach to the station by the Keeper and some citizens of Ocean City including the signal operator, a Mr. James Crawford, while the life-saving crew secured their gear. They were cared for during the next two days. The body of the sailor Anton was found sixteen miles to the south of the vessel two days later.

Pound fishermen from the Hagan Fish Company, 1906.
Courtesy of Elizabeth Gordy

Talbot Street looking west from the boardwalk in 1910. Note the sand streets and wooden sidewalks. Buildings which are the most prominent in the photograph are the Sea Crest and Mt. Vernon Hotels to the right and the Catholic Church to the left.

Courtesy of Maryland Historical Trust. Hilda Lewis Fowler Collection

A rare view of the south end of Ocean City in 1900. The boardwalk at that time was extended to South Sixth Street. The buildings are believed to be cottages belonging to the Ayres family and William Tabor. The boardwalk and the buildings were destroyed by a severe storm during September 1903 and never replaced.

Courtesy of Anne E. Englar

Fashions of the 1920s are modeled by Elizabeth Showell Strohecker, right, and friend. It was unheard of for women to go to the beach without a bathing cap or scarf.

Courtesy of Margaret Whittington

Evidence of the dedication of the personnel to the community is shown in the following two letters which were typical of many found in our research:

Mr. S. I. Kimball
General Supt. Life-Saving Service, Washington, D.C.

My Dear Sir: Representing the mayor and council of Ocean City, Md., I wish to thank you for the valuable assistance rendered to us by Captain J. B. Jones and crew of the Life-Saving Service, at the fire on September 26, 1909, which destroyed our water works and a store building in the center of our town. I believe but for their aid the greater part of our town would have been destroyed.

Very respectfully,
Francis J. Townsend
President, Mayor & Council
Ocean City

Mr. S. I. Kimball
General Supt. Life-Saving Service, Washington, D.C.

Dear Sir: It is with great gratitude that I write to you to express my thankfulness for having the life-saving station here, and for having such a good man here as Captain J. J. Dunton. He resuscitated my daughters on August 9, 1899...He worked nobly over both of them, and I owe to you and to him a debt of gratitude that I will never be able to repay.

Very truly yours,
George B. Hunting
Ocean City, 1899

Until 1930 public bathing had been confined, for the most part, to the area in front of the Life-Saving Station, under their watchful personnel. Because of severe beach erosion in this area in 1930, bathers were forced to move farther south and north. Captain William I. Purnell, chief in charge of the station, and Mayor W. W. McCabe organized a resident beach patrol of lifeguards in 1931 to protect and watch over bathers. Beginning with six members during that year, the city department has grown to over one hundred members who patrol the entire beach to the Delaware line during the summer months.

By the 1880s the Congress Hall Hotel had been built, though fire and storms prevented it from enjoying as lengthy a duration as the Atlantic Hotel. The town had also acquired a post office with two mail deliveries a week. In addition, when Colonel William Selby built the Congress Hall Hotel, guests from Philadelphia had reportedly shown an interest in establishing an Episcopal chapel; old insurance maps show a chapel near the hotel on South Division Street. Catholic interests had already been served since 1878 with the creation of a chapel, Saint Mary's Star of the Sea, at the corner of Talbot Street and Baltimore Avenue during the summer months. It became a year-round church in 1931.

Ella Phillips Dennis, with her husband Reverly, came to Ocean City in 1890 to regain her health. Finding the climate conducive and her health restored, in 1892 she built the Dennis Hotel. Mrs. Dennis was among the first women to build such an establishment on the island. Known for her outspokenness, Mrs. Dennis is quoted from an article in the *Baltimore Sun Paper* as saying, "Ocean City is seventy percent built by women, run by women and the men are all henpecked."
Courtesy of Thelma Dennis and family

Guests and staff of the Dennis Hotel posed for this picture in 1906.
Courtesy of Thelma Dennis and family

The Baltimore, Chesapeake and Atlantic Railway name began to appear locally in written records by 1888, replacing the Wicomico and Pocomoke Rail Road. Students of the railroad indicate complexities involved in the change which are not meant to be within the scope of this brief history. The B. C. & A., however, served Ocean City with efficiency, bringing visitors from Baltimore and Washington through connections with steamship facilities on the Chesapeake Bay. In addition, the trestle bridge used by the railroad to cross the Sinepuxent Bay had been designed to allow one way traffic for wagons and pedestrians. As automobile traffic increased, however, public use of rail facilities declined, resulting in the sale of the B. C. & A. at public auction in March of 1928 to the Pennsylvania system for one million dollars.

By 1890 another group of developers had formed a Baltimore-based corporation, The Sinepuxent Beach Company of Baltimore City. Its president was I. Pembroke Thom of Baltimore, and its secretary-treasurer was Frank Tuoner of Baltimore. This group purchased Taber land north and south of the existing "old town"

and expanded the subdivision approximately two miles to the south (South Thirty-Second Street), which today would be approximately opposite the development of Snug Harbor on the mainland, or Coffin's Point. They platted streets to the north as far as present-day Fifteenth Street. These boundary limitations were apparently the original lines of that parcel belonging to Stephen Taber and referred to as "Ladies Resort to the Ocean." The group created a North Division Street parallel to the downtown original Division Street (which became South Division Street). All other streets running east and west were numbered. In addition, the Sinepuxent Beach Company created a fourth north-south avenue which they named Chicago, most of which is under water today. On July 13 and 14 of 1891 they offered a grand sale of lots beginning at a cost of twenty-five dollars, with terms. Suddenly the village of Ocean City had been made nearly seven times larger in area. This corporation was eventually to purchase the original Atlantic Hotel and to lease and operate the Seaside Hotel. It was during this time that Ocean City elected its first mayor and became incorporated.

In 1896 Christopher Ludlam moved to Ocean City from New Jersey with his wife and five children. Ludlam had served as a keeper in the U. S. Life-Saving Service in New Jersey and was the recipient of the gold life-saving award medal. His arrival was significant, for he pioneered the commercial pound fishing industry in this area.

Pound fishing was a system of stationary nets attached to poles anchored in the sand of the ocean bottom. Crews would launch heavy boats capable of carrying tons of fish through the breakers of the surf and maneuver them across an outer bar to the pound areas, which were generally about a mile offshore. The nets were arranged and suspended upon large ropes, which in turn were attached to poles. A funnel-shaped net entrance allowed entry, but made escape difficult for fish. From the entrance there usually extended a long run of stationary net wall

The tranquility of village life is depicted in this photograph as men from the Mumford and Thomas Fish Company prepare the day's catch for market.
Courtesy of Mr. and Mrs. Daniel Trimper III

Susan Madora Dickerson Mason of Parksley, Virginia, came to Ocean City in 1909. The tale of her arriving in a boat with all of her possessions, including the family cow, has been a source of delight to local historians. After settling herself on the island she went into the rooming house business. Ten years later, in 1909, having established credit, she purchased the Mount Pleasant Hotel on the boardwalk at North Division Street for $10,000. Under her management the hotel became a popular and prosperous business enterprise. In 1933 she sold the hotel and retired. Susan Mason is considered one of Ocean City's pioneer women.
Courtesy of Mary Lou and Ted Brueckmann

in the direction of the beach. Fish swimming parallel to the coast line would confront the stationary wall of net and instinctively veer toward open sea or deeper water, which more often than not brought them towards the funnel opening. The fishermen usually arrived each day to work the nets, a task often made difficult by high seas and wind or the sheer weight of fish to be pulled aboard with the nets. Upon returning to the shore, they faced the difficulty of beaching the boats without capsizing them through an often-rough breaker area.

Fishing camps were built in the low area of the beach to the south of the village. During the heyday of pound fishing many such camps existed, employing many men. In addition to the Ludlam company, there were enterprises owned by Hagan, Cropper, Quillin, Davis, Lynch, Mumford, Thomas, Elliott, Belrose, Worcester, and Atlantic. The Henry E. Davis Company and the L. D. Lynch Fish Company combined after the 1933 storm (which destroyed the camps and changed the style of fishing) to form the Davis and Lynch Fish Company, the sole existing fish company of the original pound fishing industry.

Although work involved in launching the boats, working the heavy nets, tending the nets on shore, combating the elements, and beaching the boats has been described in many interviews as back-breaking and arduous, the fish camps attracted fishermen from New Jersey and the Carolinas, contributing to the growth of the village's population. The railroad had extended a line southward on the island to serve the loading platform of the fish camp as daily shipments were barreled and iced for shipment to metropolitan markets. At the end of the nineteenth century, the commercial fishing industry was a primary contributor to the economy of the town.

It has been reported that the most fish caught in one pound in one day was probably about two hundred barrels or about forty thousand pounds of fish. This was accomplished completely with manpower, since no winches, pulleys, or other machinery existed in the industry in those days. As a result, the Ocean City pound fishing crews gained reputations as experts in handling boats in rough surf conditions. An anecdote has been related to us about an all-black pound boat crew who, returning from working the nets, found the surf running quite high. Upon successfully maneuvering their boat through the monstrous waves, they were asked if they had been scared. The captain replied: "When the boat went up on one wave and we looked down, we were lookin' right down into the Berlin water tank; that's when we got scared!" This story illustrates the dangers that confronted the men working the pounds daily. Several men were known to have lost their lives, and it was not uncommon for limbs to be broken as a result of misjudging the roll of the sea between the heavy boats and the poles.

As the fish population began to decline, fewer and fewer companies continued to operate, and by the time the great storm had created the inlet in 1933, pound fishing no longer enjoyed the economic importance it had once commanded.

The turn of the century brought the era of the great hotels. Although the town already enjoyed the Atlantic, Seaside, Congress Hall, and the old original Ocean House, more hotels were built both by families already living in the town and by new families that saw a future in the resort. The large hotels had a profound influence on the character of Ocean City and in many ways guided the thinking processes of the town's leaders for half a century. By 1897 the following new hotels had been built: Belvedere Hotel, Cambridge Hotel, Colonial Hotel, Dennis Hotel, Hotel DeCropper, Eastern Shore Hotel, Isle of Wight Hotel, Seabright Hotel, Oriental Hotel, and Plimhimmon Hotel. In addition, it had become fashionable to convert larger houses and cottages into small hotels, such as Ocean Swell and the Gables. This trend continued, and by 1905 smaller hotels under the names of Belmont, Nordica, Tarry-a-While, and the Avondale were hosting guests.

The Nordica Hotel in 1906 was located at Talbot Street and the boardwalk.
Courtesy of Kathryn Jones Bunting

Charles T. Jackson, longtime engineer for the B. C. & A. Railway, in 1895.
Courtesy of Thelma Dennis and family

Baltimore, Chesapeake & Atlantic Railroad engine No. 1 on the tracks at Ocean City. The family of Thelma Jackson, whose father (above) was an engineer, posed for this 1913 photograph.
Courtesy of J. Kent Griffith

A turn-of-the-century real estate advertisement went unanswered by many. Anyone who paid the asking price during Ocean City's early development was considered out of his mind, but the buyer of yesteryear who answered this ad would, in 1978, realize an increase in his original investment of four thousand times. These lots now sell for one hundred thousand dollars minimum.

Courtesy of Elizabeth Gordy for the Showell family

Follow the Crowd

TO THE HEART OF MARYLAND

at

OCEAN CITY

The Finest Summer Resort on the Atlantic Coast

BUY LOTS WHILE THEY LAST

OCEAN AND BAY FRONT LOTS

25 x 142 feet each

PRICES: $25 and upward

$5 down, $1 per week

Discounts for Cash

Warranty Deeds   Titles Perfect

Interstate Realty Co., Inc.

OCEANIC HOTEL

BOARDWALK, OCEAN CITY, MD.

At the turn of the century, a steady program of hotel construction characterized the oceanfront properties especially, providing lodging and dining for the many vacationers who were beginning to spend longer periods of time at the resort during the summer months. Beginning in 1901 the Hamilton appeared, followed a few years later by the Mount Pleasant, Mervue, Oceanic, Windsor, Maryland Inn, Rideau, and Roosevelt. Although the First World War and the Kaiser's U-boats caused a slowdown in construction, people continued to come and enjoy the resort during this time of strife in the world. Following the war, growth continued along the same theme as before the war with the construction of the Hastings, Shoreham, Virginian, Royalton, and George Washington, followed by the Liberty Farms (later the Majestic), and Lankford. The Stephen Decatur and the Mayflower came next and were followed by the Commander. During the late 1930s the Benson and Admiral were built.

Once again, German submarines and a world at war slowed the growth of the resort. During the World War II years it was necessary to follow strict rules set forth by the government regarding lights shining seaward, amounts of food available, and gasoline consumption. Following the war, it was soon evident that a change had occurred with the vacationing public. To be sure, everything appeared as before the war. Within a few years two more large and gracious hotels were built, the Beach Plaza and the Harrison Hall. However, the public was now driving the family automobile to the resort in increasing numbers, and times were changing. Gone was the era when the host would meet his guests at the train station and care for their every need within one large gracious building, and when they would come to know each other on a personal basis. The community immediately began to address itself to newer ideas, including the concept of individual apartments, motels, and later condominiums, all of which allowed for more independence on the part of the guest.

We would be remiss if we did not take the time to review what went on behind the scenes in operating one of the larger hotels during the early history of Ocean City. Such activity, related to us by the grandchildren of some of the early prominent hotel operators, lends insight into the hardships of running such large operations while projecting the image of a happy host. Most of the older hotels were large buildings with huge capacities; the original Atlantic Hotel advertised four hundred rooms, larger than any inn today.

Materials for the original hotels were milled in Salisbury and brought by railroad to the hammocks. There they were transferred to boat or barge for transport to the island, where they were handled a third time and loaded on horse-drawn wagons to be carried to the building sites. Most lumber at that time was cut and milled green without seasoning, causing it to be much heavier than today's kiln-dried materials. Most of the hotels were covered with cedar shakes, which enjoyed long life near the coast; until the 1970s there was an obvious absence of masonry construction. Interior wall coverings were generally tongue-and-groove wainscoating or plaster over lath. The lime mixture for the plaster was mixed in large holes dug in the sand, with horsehair added for strength in application. During construction on such an isolated spot, the prevailing winds and the insects posed constant problems, and in many of the early hotels, bed netting was supplied the guest against the mosquito threat.

During the winter months, wood was cut and split in order to keep the great iron cooking stoves going in the summer. Bedding materials were mended all through the winter months, and contacts were kept with local farmers and fishermen who would supply foodstuffs. Ice had to be purchased from ice businesses that had cut it from the brackish bays the previous winter and stored it in layers of marsh grass and sawdust in large insulated rooms. With little or no refrigeration, arrangements concerning the purchase of fresh foods from local suppliers needed to be accurate since buying abilities often determined the profit on the meal, and leftovers represented loss.

Each room in the hotel had a wash bowl and pitcher for bathing, and each floor usually had a common bathroom. In addition, each room had a chamber pot. All such items had to be removed, cleaned, and returned to the rooms daily, in addition to the normal dusting and bedmaking duties.

Upon arrival in Ocean City, guests were met at the train station by a hotel porter with horse or oxen drawn wagon. Such livestock was considered an essential part of the business. It is interesting to note that as late as 1915, Ocean City felt it necessary not to allow horses, cows, oxen, sheep, or other animals to run at large or graze within the city limits unless on an enclosed lot. Hogs were completely banned from the city limits.

Pound fishing at Ocean City was introduced in 1896 by Captain Christopher Sleeper Ludlam. This industry attracted many families to make the resort their permanent residence. By the time Captain Ludlam moved to Ocean City from New Jersey, he was already the recipient of the highly coveted gold life-saving medal, an honor awarded to him for rescuing five men from a burning schooner in 1886. With his great courage and stamina, he found no trouble leading others to seek their living from the sea. Ludlam served as mayor of Ocean City from 1903 to 1908.
Courtesy of Florence DeFressine

A ride on an oxen-drawn cart was a pleasurable recreation provided for guests by
several hotels. This photograph shows
vacationers who were guests of the Belmont Hotel.
    Courtesy of Violet Cropper Davis

The first public schoolhouse on the island of Ocean City, affectionately called Marsh College by those in attendance, is shown in 1909. Located at the intersection of Philadelphia Avenue and North Division Street in a marshy area, it was later moved to Third Street and Philadelphia Avenue, where the building stands today as the Bamboo Apartments. It served elementary grades only; upper grades traveled inland for further education until Ocean City's own high school was opened in 1917. One retired teacher remembered that northeast winds caused the blackboards in the building depicted to shake. This schoolhouse might have served the community as the first theatre, for several senior citizens remember watching early picture shows in the building.

Courtesy of Mrs. Joshua Bunting
and family

Educational facilities on the island proper were nonexistent until after the turn of the century. This small structure, located in West Ocean City, served as the first schoolhouse in the area. Children walked across the railroad bridge, then approximately another one-half mile to reach the building. On Sundays the Methodists, pictured here, held Sunday School in the same building. The building, relocated and dilapidated, still stands today on Curtis Birch's Route 611 farm. It is used as a corn crib and watering trough for livestock.

Courtesy of Nannie Fisher

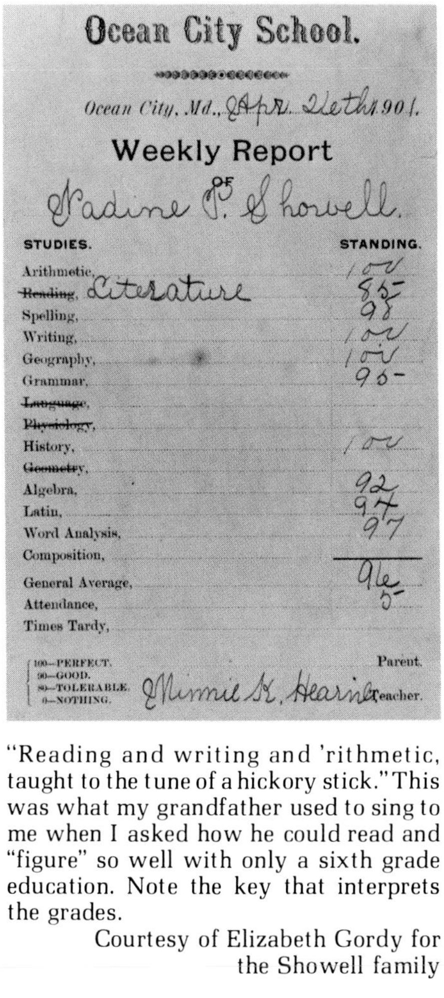

Ocean City School.

Ocean City, Md., *Apr. 26th 1901.*

Weekly Report

OF

Nadine P. Showell.

STUDIES.	STANDING.
Arithmetic,	100
~~Reading,~~ *Literature*	85
Spelling,	98
Writing,	100
Geography,	100
Grammar,	96
~~Language,~~	
~~Physiology,~~	
History,	100
~~Geometry,~~	
Algebra,	92
Latin,	97
Word Analysis,	97
Composition,	
General Average,	96
Attendance,	5
Times Tardy,	

100—PERFECT.
90—GOOD.
80—TOLERABLE.
0—NOTHING.

Parent.

Minnie K. Hearn Teacher.

"Reading and writing and 'rithmetic, taught to the tune of a hickory stick." This was what my grandfather used to sing to me when I asked how he could read and "figure" so well with only a sixth grade education. Note the key that interprets the grades.

Courtesy of Elizabeth Gordy for the Showell family

Quarters for hired help to run the hotel were generally built in the basement area, where many of the housekeeping duties originated. It was also in this area that produce was trimmed, fish cleaned, meat butchered, and hotel linen laundered by hand.

In general, it is related that the husband oversaw the operation in the basement area, including going to the fish camps for fresh fish, while the wife assumed responsibility for the kitchen, dining room, and lobby.

At the turn of the century, when the large hotels were being built in increasing numbers, it became obvious that the town needed utilities, both for practical purposes and in order to qualify for insurance coverage. When, in 1891, The Sinepuxent Beach Corporation of Baltimore sold lots to develop a portion of the island, part of the monies received from the sale had been earmarked for construction of a municipal power plant. An early reference to the plant shows that customers in 1901 were charged one dollar per light per season. In 1903 a tower tank was built in the "old town" section, as it was referred to on early Sinepuxent Beach Company plats, with water mains extending as far south as Congress Hall and north to Fifth Street. The contract also made provisions for two hand-drawn hose wagons for the nonexistent fire department.

First attempts to organize a fire company failed due to disagreements among the organizers. A second attempt in 1905 succeeded, with William B. S. Powell serving as president and Harry J. Cropper as chief. This newly formed group began holding meetings in the old Methodist Tabernacle located on Dorchester Street, which had been purchased by the city to serve as a jail and municipal building. Shortly after, it burned, and the company began to pay rent to Harry J. Cropper for storing equipment in part of his building. Through earnings from dances, plays, and suppers, the company built a new building on the site of the old one (the present site of the Ocean City Police Department). Later the Fire Department moved across the street into a new municipal building on land donated to the city by the Catholic Church. The present police building also served as City Hall until the 1960s. Today, the Fire Company's headquarters is located in the Fifteenth Street Station. The company, incorporated in 1926, is considered to be one of the best volunteer departments in the state, and is probably the largest with 125 active members, a continuing training program, a physical plant consisting of five stations, and nearly twenty pieces of the latest and most sophisticated types of fire apparatus. The company has contributed greatly over the years to the welfare of the community; besides fighting fires, it has compiled an enviable record in assistance when accidents, shipwrecks, storms, and other catastrophes have occurred.

Possibly the fire department's worst experience occurred during the Christmas holiday season of 1925. At 7:30 on a cold morning, with the wind blowing from the northwest, fire broke out in the municipal power plant at Somerset Street and Baltimore Avenue. Within minutes it was raging out of control and spreading to the nearby Seaside Hotel located directly to the

The Baltimore and Eastern Shore Railroad Station was located at South Division Street and Baltimore Avenue. Built in 1892, this station served the public until 1903. No one can remember the fate of this building.
Courtesy of Thomas I. McCabe

south of the plant. To make matters worse, the severity of the winter night had frozen the hydrants and water mains so that water to fight the fire had to be drawn from the bay. The Berlin, Snow Hill, Pocomoke, and Salisbury Fire Departments were called for assistance, and all fought the fire throughout the day. By mid-afternoon, however, the worst disaster in the town's history had occurred, with the complete loss of the power plant, the Seaside and Atlantic Hotels, the Winter Garden, the pier building and pier, Dolle's Candyland, the Casino Theatre, and two blocks of boardwalk.

By 1901 the town boasted a public school for grades one through six. It was located on the northwest corner of North Division Street and Philadelphia Avenue. Students attending this school recall that it was without facilities, but that the distance home was short. A neighbor supplied drinking water from a yard pump.

In 1915 the State Department of Education built the first section of the present City Hall building at Third Street and Baltimore Avenue. It was built to train high school graduates to become teachers, because Towson, Maryland, which was the only other institute for such training, was an inconvenient distance for residents of the Eastern Shore. After only two years in operation, the building was sold by the state to the county, and it became the first high school of Ocean City. The older elementary building was moved to Third Street and was used for a few more years in that capacity. The elementary school was sold about 1929 to private interests and stands today as the

Elizabeth Harper Hearne moved to Ocean City in 1896. Having faith that the town would prosper, she purchased in 1902 the Lambert Ayres cottage and one vacant lot on Dorchester Street. The cottage was renovated slightly and renamed the Belmont. In 1910 she built a residence next to the hotel. Mrs. Hearne, pictured here in 1900, spent most of her eighty-one years building a thriving business.
Courtesy of Kathryn Jones Bunting

36

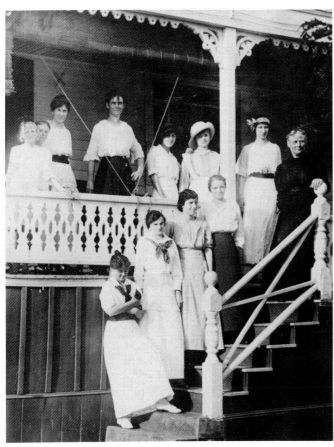

A 1916 photograph of guests and staff of the Avondale Hotel

Courtesy of Hilda Savage
for the Rounds family

This building now the home of Mr. and Mrs. James Jarman, is typical of early boarding houses on the island. Photograph 1906.

Courtesy of Hilda Savage
for the Rounds family

The Hamilton Hotel, built around the turn of the century, was located on Third Street and Atlantic Avenue. It was noted for its fine cuisine: the highlight of the week was Sunday supper, when the menu consisted of broiled chicken and waffles. Meals were enhanced by orchestra music which flowed from the music room.

Courtesy of Mr. and Mrs. William Matthews
and family

Somerset Street and the Atlantic Hotel as they appeared in 1903.
Courtesy of Ocean City Museum Society,
Helen Chandler Collection

Waiting for the flood water to recede on Dorchester Street after the 1933 storm.
Courtesy of Mrs. Joseph Elliott, Jr.

Bamboo Apartments.

The Depression years brought very difficult times in the resort. Several people recall the work of townswomen in supplying soup each day for school children who otherwise would have not eaten all day, and the presence of Civilian Conservation Corps personnel, participating in "make work" federal programs. It was during this time that the high school was enlarged. By the early 1960s all school children were attending larger, consolidated school systems on the mainland. The island's school building was later purchased by the city and is used as the City Hall building today.

Early in the century references are made to an inlet that existed south of the present inlet. It was located approximately across from the area of the municipal airport or Coffin Point area on nautical charts. It was navigable from time to time, as evidenced by North Beach Life-Saving Station Wreck Reports indicating rescues of boats trying unsuccessfully to enter it. During the late teens and early twenties there was an attempt by local businessmen to open the inlet and make it usable. Subscriptions were solicited,and work under Captain William B. S. Powell commenced in clearing it and lining it with double rows of piling with brush piled between to serve as primitive retaining walls. Much to the dismay of investors, when the surfbank was dug away, the inlet immediately closed itself again, almost within hours. Ironically, this same inlet reopened during the 1962 storm, and the government had to go to great expense to close it. Evidence of it exists today across from the Municipal Airport.

Nature, however, solved the problem of an inlet on August 23, 1933. On that date a severe northeast storm swept the resort area, leaving in its wake many damaged buildings and an inlet with deep water that was navigable almost immediately.

Baltimore Avenue and Dorchester Street in 1913. This area was the hub of the business district until the 1950s. Note the train tracks which ran on Baltimore Avenue, which had by 1913 been abandoned, but not removed. Courtesy of Maryland Historical Trust, Hilda Lewis Fowler collection

The late Dr. Charles Purnell described the storm of 1933 in *The Sunday Sun Magazine*: August 23, 1953:

It had started raining during the night and the wind was blowing hard, almost from the east. When nor'easters come, they usually cut diagonally across us and take the sand away, but this one was dumping sand right in on us. The breakers were coming straight in, too, and they'd hit the beach and pile right over into the town. By the next night there wasn't much of the storm, and the old ocean was just like she hadn't done anything; she was very innocent.

But the storm changed the face and life-style of Ocean City. The commercial fishing camps on the island to the south of town had been destroyed, and only a few tried to rebuild and continue. The town had been enjoying a fine season, and the day after the storm guests began showing up to reclaim the rooms they had vacated just two days prior. Significantly, one man and woman offered four days later to pay Captain D. Frank Parsons to take them out through the new inlet to fish offshore. Against his father's wishes he did so, little realizing that a whole new era of fishing was beginning for the town. It is a matter of conjecture as to which person first navigated the new inlet, but Parsons did help pioneer the taking of paying guests to fish in the ocean. To be sure, others had fished in the ocean from boats before, but they had been limited to those brave souls willing to risk launching through the shore break. In addition, there had, for some time, been commercial bottom fishing from boats in the waters of the Sinepuxent Bay behind the resort.

In 1905, a small convention group known as the Knockers Club posed for this photograph on the porch of the Belmont Hotel.

Courtesy of Kathryn Jones Bunting

During the season of 1934, two brothers from Selbyville, Delaware, Jack and Paul Townsend, pioneered the billfishing sport by chartering a vessel to search for marlin. It is said that commercial fishermen had often reported seeing large fish "tailing" offshore. The Townsend brothers located marlin southeast of Ocean City on the now-famous Jack Spot Shoal. The first successful angler to actually catch one was John Mickle of Florida. Frank D. Parsons relates in 1978 that "we knew they were there, but we didn't know how to fish for them. We couldn't get them to take a hook." By 1939, the local sportfishing captains had learned to hook these fish quite well, for the city was being referred to as the White Marlin Capital of the World. Today, sportfishing is a primary industry in the fabric of Ocean City's economy.

The 1933 storm had left another mark in its wake. The railroad had been dealt a severe blow: during the height of the storm, the bridge had been swept away. It was never replaced. The system of mass transit provided by the railroad had fallen into disfavor with the public and the state of Maryland had built a new highway bridge across the bay in 1916. It entered the island at Worcester Street, and since its construction and the improvement of the automobile, increasing numbers of vacationers visited the resort in their own vehicles. The train continued to serve commercial interests in West Ocean City for many years, however.

Portions of Ocean City's famous boardwalk were laid during the 1880s, and by 1897 the promenade extended to Eighth Street. The amusements which are located on the southern end of the boardwalk have for generations entertained millions of vacationers. Through the years attractions such as bowling alleys, shooting galleries, Japanese bowling, merry-go-rounds, fortune-tellers, funhouses, and games of chance have been offered to the public. Wicker rolling chairs, the famous Pier Ballroom, elegant tea rooms, a salt water bathing pool, and a band shell also added to the enjoyment of the boardwalk. Souvenir, candy, popcorn, and taffy apple concessions encouraged a carnival atmosphere. Today the boardwalk extends approximately three miles to the north of the inlet.

During the post-World War II years and the early 1950s, vast changes took place on the island. The desire for recreation and a home away from home seemed to be primary factors, with increasing numbers of young families seeking to be near the ocean for their vacations. The influx of new property owners created many changes within the town, which, until this time, had remained a typical small community during the winter months regardless of its summer population. Property values began to escalate, and many property holders, thinking the boom would end, sold tracts of land to new developers north of the town at prices relatively inexpensive by today's standards. When the state of Maryland built the Chespeake Bay Bridge, connecting the Western and Eastern Shores of the state and making the trip to Ocean City by auto less than half a day from metropolitan areas, real estate sales soared.

Josephine Lewis Massey came to Ocean City from Baltimore in the 1890s. In 1901 she purchased the partially constructed Hamilton Hotel at Third Street and the boardwalk. A refined and independent woman, she devoted the remainder of her life to making the Hamilton one of the finest hotels of its day.

Courtesy of Mrs. F. Massey Black

John Dale Showell, Sr., and Bettie West Showell were prominent in the development of Ocean City as a resort town. Moving to Ocean City in 1895, they devoted the rest of their lives to the progress and development of the resort. They operated the Mount Vernon, the Oceanic, the Essex, Showell's Theatre, and Showell's Bath House, and they were interested in many community projects. Mr. Showell served as postmaster for many years.

Courtesy of Elizabeth Gordy
for the Showell family

Squire Mumford's store was the setting for this group picture taken shortly after 1910. *Left to right:* E. M. Scott, Jim Mumford, Grover Adams, Lambert Brittingham, Alvin Townsend, Roger Adams, George Taylor, and Clarence Carey.

Courtesy of Mr. and Mrs. John B. Lynch. Jr.

The prominent John Lynch family has served the town of Ocean City since the turn of the century. Lynch was the village grocer. After his death, in 1926, his wife Minnie and son John, pictured here, built the Royalton Hotel in partnership with Ethel Kelley. In 1931, Minnie and John B. built the Commander Hotel at Fourteenth Street. The Commander continues to be owned by their descendants.
Courtesy of Marie Rickards

The lighthouse-like structure housed the water system for the Dominican Retreat, a summer home for young men studying for the priesthood. Located "out of town" between Thirteenth and Fourteenth streets, it was built before the turn of the century. The structure no longer exists.
Courtesy of Mrs. Joshua Bunting and family

During the post-war period, "motor courts," "motor hotels," and "motels" became the predominant type of construction. One noticeable difference was that these new hostelries lacked dining rooms, and thus encouraged additional construction of restaurants within the city.

During the 1950s, other changes were taking place, including the moving of the high school program from the island to the mainland, the widening of city streets, and the surfacing of others that previously were only plats on paper. The municipal disposal area was moved from the Fifteenth Street area to an inland site, and the boardwalk was extended and then extended again to accommodate the growth of oceanfront motels. During the war, a new concrete state highway bridge had been erected, entering the city at North Division Street, and the older structure to the south had been demolished, making entry onto the island much more convenient. It was during the fifties also that city leaders made decisions on at least two occasions to discourage heavy industry from settling in the immediate area. This action was taken to keep the area's environment as pollution-free as possible.

Few events in Ocean City's history compare in magnitude to the March storm of 1962. Though it was catastrophic at the time, the storm seemed to serve as a test of the city's ability to recover and rebuild itself. With the help of friends and much hard work from Ocean City citizens, the city leaders were inspired by the devastation to direct the city towards even stronger growth.

Residents of Ocean City awoke on the sixth to a hard, driving rain, but went about their daily routines. By evening, however, anxiety developed when tides became drastically high. As has been traditional, members of the volunteer fire department were unofficially assembling at the station house to lend assistance in the event the storm heightened. As feared, during the night the storm gained momentum, and the winds kept the already high tides pent up in the bay area. By morning, evacuation procedures had begun. Tides had risen eight feet above normal. As the tide went through a normal cycle, beachfront property was crushed and destroyed by the raging surf and high winds. An inlet was formed at approximately Seventieth Street, forcing firemen to stand helplessly during the height of the storm and watch property burn uncontrolled while tidal waves surged between them and the fire.

This rare photograph, circa 1900 is of the Washington Hotel which was located on Talbot Street. The hotel was also known as the Brighton and later the Cavilier.
Courtesy of Edward Hammond

When the wind and sea finally abated after three days, the destruction wrought by the storm was extensive. Whole building systems had disappeared, presumably washed to sea, with only well pipes remaining on flat, sandy lots as mute testimony to prior habitation. Other buildings lay crushed in the surf. The boardwalk was nearly destroyed. The older and larger hotels had fared better, due to their having been originally built on tall pilings many feet into the sand; however, hundreds of tons of sand filled their basements. Street systems were covered with several feet of sand, and automobiles lay buried out of sight. In all, financial loss was estimated at twenty million dollars. Two watermen had lost their lives, and one motorist died in the height of the storm in the area of the new inlet.

Almost within hours after the storm had subsided, cleanup

44

and reconstruction programs in the public and private sectors were initiated, with the assistance of state and federal government funds. New building codes provided safeguards against similar future natural catastrophes. The rebuilding programs and the temporarily deflated post-storm property values attracted new investors to Ocean City.

By 1965 the area north from Forty-Fifth Street to the Delaware line had been annexed to become a part of the municipality. Water and sewer lines were extended north to Delaware, allowing future development to continue, and the complexion of the island began to change in dramatic ways that no one could have anticipated. Whole blocks of pastel-colored cottages that had traditionally dotted the dunes of North Ocean City began to vanish as room was created for a new style of architecture: large, cube-shaped edifices of concrete, in some

Bill Gibbs slits the day's catch while his sister, Nannie Fisher, watches and her children, Everett and Helen, play in the sand. This photograph was taken in 1913 at the Atlantic Fish Company site owned by Turner Cropper and Bill Gibbs.

Courtesy of Nannie Fisher

The Glendale Hotel, 1910.
Courtesy of Doris Dennis

On December 4, 1911, the Italian ship Fortuna, heavily laden with a cargo of bones used to produce fertilizer, and bound from South America to Philadelphia, ran aground in the vicinity of Fourteenth Street. Twenty persons were rescued through the combined efforts of the Ocean City and Isle of Wight Life-Saving Stations, The Ship was later floated off and her crew returned on board.
Courtesy of Melville Quillin

instances towering twenty-two stories into the sky and housing multiple independent living units under one roof system. These condominium complexes could not be built fast enough for the buyers who were waiting to purchase them during the early seventies, and, in fact, it has been reported that many such buildings were sold out before the ground had been broken for construction. A striking result is a comparison of population figures during winter months of less than five thousand compared to about an average of 150,000 on a typical summer day, with the figures increasing each year.

Dramatic transformations have characterized the evolution of Ocean City from a small fishing village to a major seaside resort. Progressive change has steadily occurred; new ideas are constantly being introduced through continuing assimilation of new residents, and those already here seek conscientiously to safeguard the beauty and future of the city. Occasionally nature speeds change along, using coastal storms as catalytic agents, or man retards the pace through international incidents such as war.

But the tradition of gracious hospitality and the timeless lure of the sea are unchanged from John Dos Passos' description of Ocean City in the 1870s, when "up in the little pine bedroom...the roar of the surf came in through the rusty screen...."

A group of young people pose in front of the Seaside Hotel in 1910.
Courtesy of Mrs. Joshua Bunting
and family

A postcard photograph of Lilly Williams Elliott, left, and Ella Brittingham Taylor Quillin taken in 1915. Descendants of both women are today prominent Ocean City business people.

Courtesy of George and Suzanne Hurley

Captain William B. S. Powell, an extensive landholder, was prominent in Ocean City's early development. He was first president of Ocean City's volunteer fire company in 1905; keeper of Green Run Life-Saving Station, 1902–1909, and North Beach Life-Saving Station, 1909–1911; and Ocean City's eighth mayor 1912–1916.

Courtesy of Thelma Dennis and family

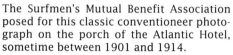

The Surfmen's Mutual Benefit Association posed for this classic conventioneer photograph on the porch of the Atlantic Hotel, sometime between 1901 and 1914.

Courtesy of Florence DeFressine

Relatives and friends of the William Collins family on the beach at Ocean City in 1913. Left to right, standing: Mattie Truitt, Arthur Lee Collins, Ruth Farlow, unknown, Vivian Collins, Leland Truitt (married). Left to right, seated: Berdie McNeal Marshall, Roxie May Baker Collins.

Courtesy of William Collins

On the night of March 12, 1912, the schooner *John W. Hall*, 346 tons, bound from Wilmington, North Carolina, to New York City, lost her bearings and ran into shoal water three miles south of Ocean City. Mary Bunting posed near the vessel shortly before it became a total loss.
Courtesy of Mrs. Joshua Bunting and family

The *John W. Hall* lies stranded in the surf. Her crew of seven men was rescued and housed at the Ocean City Life-Saving Station. The cargo of lumber, also saved, is to the left in the photograph. It is interesting to note that of the thirty-four lives saved on the Del-Mar-Va coast during the fiscal year July 1, 1911, to May 30, 1912, twenty–seven were rescued by the surfmen of the Ocean City Station. Young children, such as those pictured, used the vessel as a temporary playground.
Courtesy of Violet Cropper Davis

The Laurel Cottage as it appeared in 1910. The small hotel was located on the corner of Dorchester Street and the Boardwalk.
Courtesy of Maryland Historical Society, Hilda Lewis Fowler collection

A deserted boardwalk on a stormy day in September 1919. The pier building, Dolle's Candyland and the Glendale Hotel are featured in this photograph.
Courtesy of Marge Seim

An early photograph of Trimper's Luna Park, shown before it was destroyed by the storm of 1933. The building in the left is Congress Hall, one of the first hotels on the island, which burned in 1927. Today, Windsor Resort Corporation, of which Luna Park was a portion, encompasses a large section of the downtown amusement area, which includes the oldest operating merry-go-round in the United States.
Courtesy of
Mr. and Mrs. Daniel Trimper III

Saint Mary's Star of the Sea Catholic Church was the first church built in the newly developed town. Church records are not quite clear, but 1878 appears to be the accepted date. It can be speculated that many early summer vacationers were devout Catholics who required a house of worship, since there were no Catholic families living on the island until 1920. Today there are three Catholic churches to accommodate the increasing winter population and the summer vacationers. Photograph, 1912.
Courtesy of Elizabeth Gordy
for the Showell family

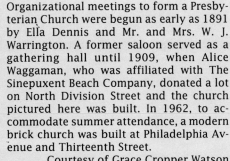

Organizational meetings to form a Presbyterian Church were begun as early as 1891 by Ella Dennis and Mr. and Mrs. W. J. Warrington. A former saloon served as a gathering hall until 1909, when Alice Waggaman, who was affiliated with The Sinepuxent Beach Company, donated a lot on North Division Street and the church pictured here was built. In 1962, to accommodate summer attendance, a modern brick church was built at Philadelphia Avenue and Thirteenth Street.
Courtesy of Grace Cropper Watson

Daniel Trimper, Sr., played an influential role in the growth and development of the resort. Trimper, his wife, Margaret, and their ten children built the famous Windsor Resort, an amusement park located near today's inlet. The complex was a major attraction for visitors at the turn of the century, and remains so today.
Courtesy of The Daily Times, Inc.

Susie Amanda Rounds was a prominent and highly respected hotel owner. Mrs. Rounds and her husband George moved to the resort in 1904 and began receiving paying guests into their home. In 1914 the family traded their home for the Avondale Hotel. Later they purchased the Del-Mar-Va Hotel and remained at that location for twenty–five years. After her husband's death, Mrs. Rounds bought the newly constructed Liberty Farms Hotel in the early 1940', renaming it the Majestic. Her life was devoted to the betterment of the community and the growth of the hospitality industry.
Courtesy of Hilda Savage
for the Rounds family

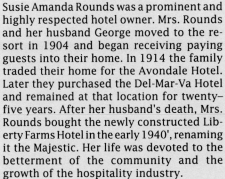

The original Colonial Hotel, shown in 1915, was located between Second and Third streets on the boardwalk.
    Courtesy of Mr. and Mrs. Alan Quillin

The Avondale Hotel, located on Talbot Street and Baltimore Avenue, is shown in 1918.
    Courtesy of Hilda Savage
    for the Rounds family

W. Preston Laws posed for this postcard photograph upon his enlistment during World War I. Laws was always an interested and active leader in the community.

Courtesy of Kathryn Laws

A boardwalk scene, taken in 1912, shows a lifeboat on the sand.

Courtesy of Elizabeth Gordy
for the Showell family

During the winter of 1914, these two gentlemen, Lyle R. Cropper, *right*, and his friend Jack Bunting, *left*, paused for a photograph on Ocean City's ice-covered beach.

Courtesy of Mr. and Mrs. George Hurley

In 1913 a Curtis Flying Boat attracted a curious crowd when it landed on Sinepuxent Bay. The aviator possibly landed to have lunch and show off his new flying machine. The photograph was taken on South Division Street and the bay.

Courtesy of D. Frank Parsons and Ocean City Museum Society

An early kindergarten class assembled in the basement of the Presbyterian Church in 1914.
Courtesy of
Mr. and Mrs. Hugh T. Cropper, Jr.

Clarence Carey, *left*, displays a pitiful looking string of fish. The man at right is unidentified.
Courtesy of Doris Dennis

Madam Carrie Stanley reigned supreme during the heyday of fortune-telling on the boardwalk. An English gypsy, Madam Stanley was allowed to remain in business when others of her profession were banned from the resort. A loyal patron, Thomas J. Cropper, poses with her in 1915.
Courtesy of Violet Cropper Davis

Only a few vacationers remain on the boardwalk in this late September 1919 photograph.

Courtesy of Marge Seim

This gentleman's picture was found in many of the photograph collections we searched. Thinking he was prominent in the community history, we had several reproduced only to discover his claim to fame was that he had only one finger. His name was Billy McKue.

Courtesy of Violet Cropper Davis

At the turn of the century, Ocean City's Post Office was not only used for sending and receiving mail, but as a place for congregating and passing the time of day. *Standing, left to right*: Ned Purnell, Neal Coffin, Bob Quillin, Paul Coffin, Grover Adams, Ned Hastings, Sam Monkhouse, unidentified, Asa Quillin, Horace Quillin, and Bill Brittingham. *Seated, left to right*: Reverly Dennis, Jess Truitt, unidentified, Sammy Monkhouse, and Harold Rayne, Sr. The building no

Courtesy of Mrs. Joshua Bunting
and family

This photograph shows the entrance into Ocean City during 1920. The automobile bridge entered the town at Worcester Street.
Courtesy of the Ocean City Museum Society, Louise Chambliss collection

The main street into Ocean City as it appeared in 1920. This photograph shows the intersection of Worcester Street and Baltimore Avenue. Both street front buildings are still standing. To the left, the garage is today Gentleman Jim's and the "rooms for rent" building is an apartment house. The boardwalk buildings are today so altered structurally that they are unrecognizable.
Courtesy of the Ocean City Museum Society, Louis Chambliss collection

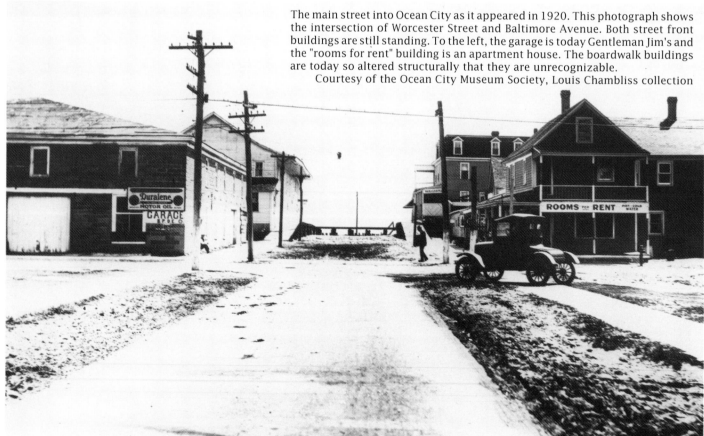

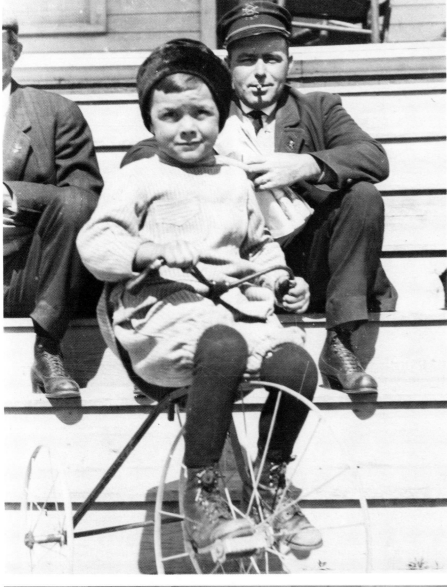

John B. Jones is pictured here with his son Hearne. He was the keeper of the Ocean City Life-Saving Station from 1907 until 1917.
Courtesy of Kathryn Jones Bunting

Five crew members of the United States Revenue Cutter *Yamacraw* survived a tragic rescue operation during the night of March 4, 1917. Eleven other crew members perished in an attempt to rescue the crew of the *Louisiana*, a United States tanker, aground on a reef one and one-half miles due east of Ocean City. The details of this incident are too bizarre and lengthy to expound upon here; except to note, there was no loss of life on the tanker in distress. *Yamacraw* crew members, Winn, McWilliams, Fiddler, and Miller are in the photograph. Hogarth, left, a seventeen–year–old cabin boy can be identified.
Courtesy of D. Frank Parsons and
Ocean City Museum Society

Joseph Schaefer

WHOLESALE AND RETAIL

ICE CREAM

DEALER

BAKER AND

CONFECTIONER

DELICATESSEN

Out of Town Orders Promptly Filled

BALTIMORE AVE. & SOMERSET ST., OCEAN CITY, MD.

Denward Collins Ayres and his sister Amanda
Virginia, children of Samuel J. and Dellie Ayres,
posed for this photograph in 1924. Special
places were marked along the boardwalk to
document the moment.
Courtesy of Michael Day from the collection
of Virginia Ayres Satterfield

BOARDWALK, OCEAN CITY, MD.

An agent with the Baltimore, Chesapeake
and Atlantic Railway, Edward M. Scott was
the founder of the first telephone company
on the island and served as mayor of the
town from 1918 to 1920. He is pictured
with his son William.
Courtesy of
Mr. and Mrs. Daniel Trimper III

Pony rides on the beach were a favorite attraction for the young. Captain William B. S. Powell and Joe Hickmont rented ponies for ten cents per half-hour. This photograph was taken in front of the Oceanic Hotel on the boardwalk at North Division Street.
Courtesy of Thelma Dennis and family

Wetipuin Hall, located between Second and Third streets on the boardwalk. Courtesy of Mr. and Mrs. William Matthews and family

Robert J. Fisher is pictured on Third Street in 1919 with his Holly Grove Farm Dairy wagon. Fresh milk and butter were brought in daily to the hotels and boarding houses. Mrs. Fisher reminisces that business improved the following year when they retired "Old Tom" and bought a car, enabling them to make more trips into town.

Courtesy of Nannie Fisher

Flying Jennies, World War I-vintage aircraft, in 1920 caused curious crowds to assemble on the bay shore of the island. Such events were cause enough in a rural village to allow normal work activities to stop in order to take advantage of the moment.

Courtesy of Annie Quillen and family

The pier building collapsed from the weight of snow and ice in 1918. At that time ocean waters washed under the building on normal tides. The building at the end of the pier was the Dancing Pavilion, considered to be quite luxurious. The structure was rebuilt and in operation for the 1918 summer season.

Courtesy of Violet Cropper Davis

The Mount Pleasant Hotel was located on the Boardwalk between North Division and First streets. Built in 1900 by Margaret Campbell Buell, the hotel saw several different owners through its sixty-year history. In the early 1970s the hotel burned to the ground,
Courtesy of the Ocean City Museum Society

The Hastings Hotel, pictured in 1923, was built by Josephine Hastings and later became the property of Willye Jones Conner Ludlam. The hotel was demolished in 1975 to increase parking facilities in the area.
Courtesy of Mr. and Mrs. William Matthews and family

The Seaside Hotel, one of the first three hotels built on the island prior to 1874, was unique: it was not an oceanfront hotel. Located on Baltimore Avenue and Wicomico Street, it was built by Samuel Massey of Berlin, Maryland. Early advertising for the hotel states that rooms were two dollars a day or ten dollars a week; meals were fifty cents each, with liberal arrangements made for families. The hotel boasted a first-class bar, bowling alley, and livery stable. The Seaside Hotel, photographed in 1923, burned in 1925 and was never rebuilt.
Courtesy of Mr. and Mrs. Alan Quillin and family

Willye Jones came to the resort near the turn of the century seeking work for the summer. She met and married George Conner, owner of Conner's Restaurant, an established business since the late 1880s. She became the mother of three children and shortly thereafter was widowed. Mrs. Conner continued to manage the business until 1922, when she had the opportunity to sell the restaurant and purchase the newly built Hastings Hotel and cottage. Mrs. Conner married Charles Ludlam, who was instrumental in the early pound fishing industry. By the early 1940s, recognizing Ocean City's growth potential, she bought and built several more important houses. In 1965 she built one of the town's first motels, the Santa Maria.

Courtesy of Mr. and Mrs. Milton Conner

During World War I, many of Ocean City's residents served in the United States Coast Guard, patrolling and guarding the coastline. Pictured here is the crew of the North Beach Coast Guard Station during a drill in 1918. *Left to right*: Captain Henry Richardson, Thomas Moore, William Burbage, Levin Bunting, Jr., Ebe Elliott, E. King, Edwin Taylor, unidentified reservist. The above crew participated in the rescue of sixty–five seamen aboard the American freighter *Saetia*, which hit a German mine and sank twenty–five miles off Assateague Island on November 9, 1918.

Courtesy of Mrs. Edwin Taylor

Harry G. Parsons, flagman with the B. C. & A., worked on the freight line which ran to Claiborne, Maryland.
Courtesy of D. Frank Parsons and Ocean City Museum Society

In 1920 a group of vacationers poses with the day's catch at the foot of Jarvis Pier, located on Wicomico Street and the bay. Jarvis Pier was built by Raymond Jarvis, Sr. The pier was destroyed during the storm of 1933.
Courtesy of Melville Quillin

The loading platform ran along the railroad on the island, beginning at South First Street, through all of the fish companies. In this 1918 photograph, a group of workmen congregate on the platform.

Courtesy of Etta Cropper Davidson

Steve Quillin, Sr., was an engineer on the Baltimore, Chesapeake and Atlantic freight train originating from the fish camps in Ocean City.

Courtesy of Mr. and Mrs. Alan Quillin and family

A view of the train station which was located on the corner of Philadelphia Avenue and Somerset Street during the 1920s. The horse and baggage cart awaiting the Baltimore Flyer's arrival was a familiar scene. The depot was built in 1903 when the railroad tracks were moved from Baltimore Avenue to Philadelphia Avenue to alleviate congestion along the town's main street. In 1933, rail service into Ocean City was halted when the rail bridge was destroyed during a hurricane. The depot was moved to a new location between Talbot and Dorchester streets on Philadelphia Avenue and today serves as a warehouse.

Courtesy of Josiah and Madlyn Bethards

A paradise for duck hunters, the marshes behind Ocean City and Assateague Island draw scores of sportsmen from the cities. Houseboats, better known as "gunning shacks," provided sleeping bunks, meals, and a good night of poker. The duck blinds were reached with small skiffs. There was no bag limit, and any excess fowl were shipped to Baltimore and Philadelphia markets.

Courtesy of Melville Quillin

As early as 1881 a small church building had been erected near the Congress Hall Hotel for the many Episcopalian vacationers and investors of the original town. This first land was donated by Steven Taylor. Robert Showell of Berlin, Maryland, conducted regular Sunday School services during its early development. In 1898 John F. Waggaman donated two lots an Baltimore Avenue and Third Street for the building of a new Episcopal Church. When Christopher Ludlam bought the old church property, the proceeds of the sale were used to build a new church, constructed in 1899 and dedicated in 1900 as Saint Paul's-by-the-Sea Episcopal Church. Many of Ocean City's first families participated in the early development and growth of the church. The original church and a sister church built at One-Hundredth Street today serve the expanding summer population of the city. This photograph was taken in 1915.

Courtesy of Ellen Lynch Weaver

Priests attending the summer school for the Dominican Brotherhood of the Catholic University, Washington, D.C., pose for this 1925 photograph.

Courtesy of Barbara Gill

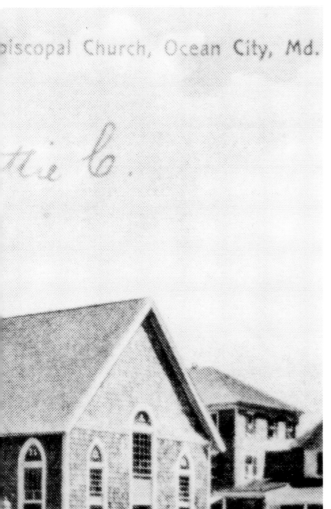

piscopal Church, Ocean City, Md.

Buildings such as this one provided sleeping quarters and three-squares-a-day to personnel at the fish camps. Breakfast was served at 4 a.m. lunch at 10 a.m., and supper at 3 in the afternoon.. The men were paid seven dollars a week, which was considered fair wages in 1915.

Courtesy of Grace Cropper Watson

Written on the back of this rare fish camp picture was this description: "Catch, April 30, 1917, Worcester Fish Company, Ninety–three bushels."

Courtesy of Otho Taylor and family

The Tarry-A-While, a small hotel, is located on Dorchester Street on the oceanside. Built before the turn of the century, the hotel could accommodate twenty–five guests. This business has remained in the hands of the Davis-Cropper family for over ninety years. Note that in 1920 the business was advertising running water in each room.
Courtesy of Violet Cropper Davis

Prince, the favorite horse of Thomas Q. Cropper, went out of this world in grand style. Horses in those days were considered working members of a family and were apparently given as much respect at death. This photograph was taken on Baltimore Avenue at Somerset Street in 1915.
Courtesy of Etta Cropper Davidson

In 1917 Ralph Dennis, Ocean City's first male principal, posed with his students. Not only was Dennis instrumental in the education of the town's youth, but he also played a large role in the formation of the volunteer fire company in 1905, serving as its first assistant chief. He was the only member in the history of the company to lose his life while fighting a fire.

Courtesy of Thelma Dennis and family

Naomi K. Workman was a most respected and loved woman of Ocean City. Paralyzed as a young girl from polio, she did not let this deter her activeness. She served the local telephone company as its head operator until her death in the early 1960s and never left her post during disasters such as the hurricanes which frequently swept the coast during her lifetime. Miss Workman was awarded the Vale Medal for Bravery in 1921.

Courtesy of Etta Cropper Davidson

This lovely old photograph depicts the mode of travel to and from Ocean City in the early 1900s. It is said that on Sundays the bay was full of small craft originating from the rivers and creeks which flowed into the Sinepuxent Bay from the mainland. J. W. Quillin is shown here with his family in 1920.

Courtesy of Melville Quillin

George Rounds purchases fresh fish to be served at his hotel for the evening meal.

Courtesy of Hilda Savage
for the Rounds family

Thomas J. and Sallie Cropper, early entrepreneurs of the community, pose with their daughter Violet, *left*, and grandchildren for this 1920 photograph in front of one of the family businesses.

Courtesy of
Mr. and Mrs. Hugh T. Cropper, Jr.

76

There are no exact records of the origins of Methodism in Ocean City, but in 1897 there was a Methodist Tabernacle located on Dorchester Street. Around 1905, the city bought the building, and the congregation met at various places until 1919, when the church pictured here was built on Fourth Street and Baltimore Avenue. Demolished in 1962, it was replaced with a large brick church to accommodate the growing summer population.

Courtesy of Mr. and Mrs. Alan Quillin

The Del-Mar-Va Hotel during the 1930s. Built by Josephine Hastings, the hotel was originally named the Avelon Hotel. Located on First Street and Baltimore Avenue, it was well known for its fine Eastern Shore cuisine.

Courtesy of Hilda Savage
for the Rounds family

Dr. Charles Purnell, Ocean City business-man, bought the Atlantic Hotel in 1923, just prior to its destruction by fire in 1925. He rebuilt the structure and operated the hotel until his death in 1961.

Courtesy of Charles D. Purnell

Elisha Victor Bunting was Ocean City's first recipient of the gold life-saving medal. The award was presented in August of 1926, after Bunting had rescued four men from drowning when their fishing boat had overturned in a rough and dangerous sea. Life-saving medals are bestowed only upon those who risk their lives above and beyond the call of duty.

Courtesy of Lilly Farlow for the Bunting family

The beach at North Division Street in 1924. Note the height of the boardwalk at that time. Betty and Brevard D. Strohecker are in the foreground.

Courtesy of Elizabeth (Betty) Gordy for the Showell family

Edgar C. Gaskins was a prominent merchant dealing in general merchandise. His store was located on the corner of Talbot and Baltimore Avenue.
Courtesy of Mr. and Mrs. Edgar Gaskins and family

Charles A. Parker, left, and William Burbage, career men of the Coast Guard stationed at Ocean City.
Courtesy of Mr. and Mrs. Mike Parker

An early photograph, probably taken during the 1920s, shows the U.S. Coast Guard Station in Ocean City, located at Caroline Street and Atlantic Avenue (boardwalk). Early Life-Saving Service records indicate that its personnel participated in many heroic rescues during the era of sailing vessels. Many of the men stationed here figured prominently in the town's development. This building, presently renovated as a municipal museum, was constructed in 1891. In this rare photograph, the original station house built in 1878 is shown to the left. The Victorian style of architecture is evidenced in both buildings. The building is listed officially in the National Archives as being located "on the northern edge of the village."

Courtesy of Kathryn Jones Bunting

Levin J. Bunting, Jr., was awarded the highly coveted gold life-saving medal for "rescuing a woman and a young girl from the perils of the sea" in 1924. The award was presented at the Atlantic Hotel during August of 1928.

Courtesy of Mrs. Levin J. Bunting, Jr.

Top: Looking north from Surf Avenue in 1926.

Bottom: Baltimore Avenue at Seventh Street in 1926. The Liberty Farms hotel had just been completed the year before. The flow of traffic was two-way on Baltimore Avenue and vacationers and locals alike complained, then as they do today, about the congestion.

Courtesy of the
Ocean City Museum Society

Wearing hand-me-down Washington Senators uniforms, the Dominican Brothers' baseball team posed for this group photograph in the early 1930s. *Left to right, first row*: B. McGivire, C. Dore, T. English, W. Farrell; *second row*: A. Fincel, H. Rayne, A. McCabe, J. Campbell; *third row*: A. Geevges, I. Litzinger, E. Rocks, P. McEvoy.

Courtesy of Manna Rayne

Elizabeth Showell Strohecker models a 1920s bathing suit. Mrs. Strohecker was a prominent businesswoman in Ocean City. After taking over the family businesses along with her brother, John D. Showell, Jr., she also extended her personal holdings. She quietly saw to the education of several young people of the town. Door-to-door mail delivery was initiated by her when she served as assistant postmaster to Ocean City in 1917.

Courtesy of Elizabeth Gordy for the Showell family

Dolle's as it looked just prior to the fire which devastated the building in 1925. The building was rebuilt in 1926, and was demolished to make way for a more modern structure in 1978. The business is still owned and operated by descendants of Rudolph Dolle.

Courtesy of Rudolph Dolle, Jr., and family

The Blue Lattice Inn, an early tea room located at North Division Street and the boardwalk, was operated by Elizabeth Showell Strohecker. The photograph was taken in 1926.
Courtesy of Elizabeth Gordy for the Showell family

The Presbyterian Men's Bible group in 1920. *Left to right, top row:* Lyle Cropper, William Lewis, Raymond Coffin, Harry Cropper, Thomas Spencer, Harry Bunting; *second row:* William Taylor, Horace Richardson, Sewell Jones, Jason Hassen, William Brittingham, Robert Quillin; *third row:* Thomas Q. Cropper, Samuel Johnson, Samuel Monkhouse, Franklin Truitt, William Rounds, Thomas Parsons; *fourth row:* Franklin Tyre, William Parker, Arthur Monkhouse, Willard Haymon, Mr. Gessley; *fifth row:* Reverend Nelson Riddle, Granville Cropper, James Savage, unidentified, John Lynch, Sr., Charles Jackson, Thomas Elliott.
Courtesy of Etta Cropper Davidson

A pound fisherman from the Levin D. Lynch Fish Company transferring his catch into baskets to be weighed and shipped to Baltimore and points north. The horse and cart in the background conveyed the baskets to the railway platform.
Courtesy of Mr. and Mrs. Mike Parker

Pound fishermen posed for this photograph on a calm day at sea in 1923.
Courtesy of Laura Parsons

The pound fishing crew of the Cropper
Fish Company in 1924.
　　　Courtesy of Etta Cropper Davidson

Rudolph and Vashti Dolle are pictured in
1922 inside the family confectionery.
Together they made from secret family
recipes their famous saltwater taffy,
fudge, and caramel corn.
Courtesy of Rudolph Dolle, Jr., and family

"Queen of the Female Swimmers," 1924,
was Elizabeth S. Elgin.
            Courtesy of Kathryn Jones Bunting

Savannah, right, and Captain Ned Carey, left, stand in front of the Del-Mar Hotel in the early 1920s. Miss Savannah was known for her famous kitchen and generous hospitality at the hotel, located on North Division Street near the boardwalk.

Courtesy of Thelma Dennis and family

A bathing scene during the 1920s.
Courtesy of Ocean City Museum Society

This aerial photograph of Ocean City shows the town in 1926 or early 1927 and the advent of the inlet. Some local people wished to establish an inlet south of the town, and Mother Nature settled the issue on August 23, 1933, by creating one roughly where the L-shaped deck appears on the right center of the photograph. Using the State Highway Bridge which entered Ocean City on Worcester Street as a reference, the reader can see that the town extended approximately to North Eighth Street during the 1920s. Approximately South Fourth Street is included in the extreme right portion of the photograph. The railroad bridge (lower bridge) entered town at South Division Street.

Courtesy of Reese Cropper, Sr., Collection

A military observation blimp draws a fascinated group of onlookers in 1925.
Courtesy of Annie Quillen and family

The Stephen Decatur Hotel was located on the boardwalk at Twelfth Street.
Courtesy of Mr. and Mr. Alan Quillin

Frank Sacca's band entertains boardwalk crowds during the 1920s.
Courtesy of Doris Dennis

Maryland's "superior" State Road and the Herring Creek Bridge, just west of Ocean City, as it appeared in 1926.
    Courtesy of Ocean City Museum Society

The Scarboro & Phine Tomato Cannery was a thriving business in the Ocean City area in 1916. The cannery was located on the bay, near today's entrance to the commercial harbor.
    Courtesy of Josiah and Madlyn Bethards

A herd of cattle belonging to William B. S. Powell was left to forage Assateague Island during the winter of 1936.
    Courtesy of Mary Adeline Bradford

This rare photograph of Ocean City's White pumper was taken after the 1925 fire.
Courtesy of Hilda Savage
for the Rounds family

A physical fitness class is conducted on the beach during the 1930s.
Courtesy of Ocean City Museum Society

William W. McCabe served as mayor of the community from 1922 to 1934. He promoted the resort by personal visits to large cities.

Courtesy of Hilda Savage for the Rounds family

The heroine of John Barth's Lost in the Funhouse today stands dejected and in a state of disrepair in a cluttered shed. During her heyday as a major boardwalk attraction, Laughing Sal delighted millions. Barth called her "Fat May the Laughing Lady," and described her thus: "Larger than life, Fat May mechanically shook, rocked on her heels, slapped her thighs while recorded laughter—uproarious, female—came amplified from a hidden loudspeaker. It chuckled, wheezed, wept: turned in vain to catch its breath: tittered, groaned, exploded raucous and anew. You couldn't hear it without laughing yourself no matter how you felt." She was owned and operated by the Lloyd Jester family.

Courtesy of Irma Jester

During Prohibition the Eastern Shore, along with most of the Atlantic Seaboard, was involved in the now famous Rum Wars. In late December of 1929, members of the Ocean City Coast Guard stand watch over 250,000 dollars worth of confiscated liquors.

Courtesy of Annie Quillen and family

This stockpile of whiskey was part of a shipment taken just south of Ocean City and trucked to the Caroline Street Station House. In 1929 it was not uncommon for such shipments to be unloaded near the surf in the night, transported by horse and cart across the island, and boated across the bay for truck transportation to inland points. In this instance, an off-duty constable on an early morning fishing jaunt to the island suspected the activity on the beach and informed the Coast Guard. Many humorous stories regarding this and other, similar occurrences during the Rum War are still told, and even today are handled delicately for fear of opening old social wounds.

Courtesy of Annie Quillen and family

Part of the cache of liquor after it was moved from the point of capture to the Coast Guard Station. There was an old saying among the Guard, "If you weren't rescuing 'em, you were arresting 'em." It must be stated that loyalties were split among the townspeople. Rum-runners were held in high regard, for they, too, were respected local men. Those who were arrested were taken from their jail cells three times daily and fed in one of the nicest hotels of the day.

Courtesy of Mrs. Joshua Bunting and family

These cases of whiskey, gin, and champagne were intended to help Washington, Baltimore, and Philadelphia make New Year's whoopee. Although the contraband was heavily guarded, it is said that most Ocean City residents, to the chagrin of the Coast Guard, had a very Happy New Year.

Courtesy of Annie Quillen and family

Sebron and Ada Hastings Gaskins Cox, owners of the Rideau Hotel in 1931.
Courtesy of Mr. and Mrs. William Matthews and family

Elbridge E. Collins, mayor of Ocean City from 1920 to 1922.

Courtesy of William Collins

Their vacation over, the Leaverton family is all packed up and ready to head home. This photograph was taken during August of 1918.
Courtesy of the Robert Leaverton family

Levin Bunting, Sr., owner of the *Princeton* and Mr. Faust, owner of the *Melinda,* pose in 1928 after being awarded the Sailing Cups for that year.
Courtesy of Mrs. Joshua Bunting and family

Parcel post deliveries were being made on the boardwalk in 1929 by Everett Fisher. In the mid-thirties Fisher opened his now-famous Fisher's Pop Corn Stand, the delight of boardwalk gourmets.
Courtesy of Nannie Fisher

The Ocean City Beach Patrol during the summer of 1931. Edward Lee Carey, *standing, center,* was captain. Joe Bunting, *seated, center,* has been identified. Henry Foster, Sam Temple, Lou Malencrodt, and Ned Dukehart are also in the photograph. The picture was taken in front of the Caroline Street Coast Guard Station, whose personnel until that time had protected and watched over swimmers. Because of beach erosion at this location, bathers were using the beach farther away from the station site, and this prompted the mayor, W. W. McCabe, and the chief of the station, W. I. Purnell, to organize the Beach Patrol to better watch over the expanding bathing area.

Courtesy of Mrs. Joshua Bunting and family

Mayor William W. McCabe with his new 1927
Chevrolet parked on the boardwalk in front of
the Fountain of Youth, a popular soda fountain and novelty store.
Courtesy of Dorothy H. Taylor

Members of the Isle of Wight Coast Guard crew in 1930. *Left to right, top row:* Willis Hudson, Samuel Quillen, Corb Gibbs, Harry Kelley; *bottom row:* Wilmer Cropper, Bancroft Williams, unidentified, Charles Massey.
Courtesy of Annie Quillen and family

The interior of the Pier Ball Room was photographed in 1931 during the first Life Guard Hop. Most of the big bands of the nation preformed here, including Tommy Dorsey, Guy Lombardo, and Harry James.
Courtesy of Mrs. Joshua Bunting and family

One of the most valued photographs ever taken in Ocean City shows the end of an era and the beginning of a new dimension for the town. On August 23, 1933, a vicious hurricane swept the Atlantic Coast. In its wake, and the surge tides that followed, the inlet was formed. Commercial fishing camps which dominated that area were leveled, and the railroad bridge linking Ocean City to the mainland was destroyed.

Courtesy of Reese Cropper, Sr., Collection

Rescue operation by the Coast Guard
during the 1933 storm.
Courtesy of Mrs. Joseph Elliott, Jr.

Evacuation of Ocean City residents.
Courtesy of Eastern Shore Times, Inc.

The sportfishing docks were heavily
damaged.
Courtesy of Mrs. Joshua Bunting
and family

This was the Whip amusement building.
Courtesy of Kathryn Jones Bunting

The fish camps which had flourished
since the late 1890s were the focal point of
the hurricane's wrath. The H. Davis camp
is pictured here after the storm abated.
Courtesy of Kathryn Jones Bunting

Proprietors of the amusement section of
the boardwalk opened for business as
usual shortly after the storm subsided.
We were delighted to find this photograph of Nathan Rappaport's building
which housed the "live mouse races."
Courtesy of Mr. and Mrs.
Daniel Trimper III

Notations on the back of this photograph are: "Herring Hog, harpooned off Ocean City, Md., 250 pounds, (party) Mr. and Mrs. T. J. Burke, Jr., July 5, 1934."
Courtesy of Mrs. Joshua Bunting and family

Captain D. Frank Parsons was the first person to challenge the new inlet, six days after it was cut. In an interview Captain Parsons said he was highly criticized, even by his father, for doing such a "dumb and dangerous thing," but "a party was willing to pay good money to fish in the ocean, and I wasn't about to turn that down." The inset shows *Little Katherine*, first party boat to pass through the inlet.
Courtesy of D. Frank Parsons and Ocean City Museum Society

FRANK PARSONS

KATHERINE
OCEAN CITY,

The Ocean City Volunteer Fire Department posed for a picture on the Atlantic Hotel lot in the early 1930s with its new American LaFrance pumper. Officers at this time were; Captain W. I. Purnell, president; Ralph R. Dennis, chief; Archie Davis, assistant chief; Herman Parsons, secretary; Lloyd Jester, treasurer.

Courtesy of Ocean City
Volunteer Fire Department

112

Virginia Dale Ayres Swindler was Ocean City's first female realtor, owning Ayres Reality. Note the large key ring at her side, which held keys to almost every apartment in town. Courtesy of Mary Lou and Ted Brueckmann

Local beauties on the Eastern Shore Prosperity Tour, in 1934, were photographed in the White House grounds in Washington, D.C. *Left to right:* Elizabeth Coffin; Grace, Arietta, Frances, and Marietta Cropper, Una Palmer.
Courtesy of Grace Cropper Watson

Captain Crawford Savage played an influential role in the development of sportfishing at the resort. He is pictured with baseball's famous Jimmy Fox, *left*, who caught his first marlin aboard the *Hil-Da* in the late 1930s.
Courtesy of Hilda Savage
for the Rounds family

The brothers Jack and Paul Townsend, wealthy businessmen from Delaware, are given full credit for the discovery of the first white marlin off the coast of Ocean City. Though a gentleman from Florida actually caught the first white marlin, it is locally acknowledged that had it not been for the Townsend brothers, sportfishing off Ocean City would not have developed until a much later date. This 1937 photograph includes, *left to right*: Paul Townsend, Captain Bill Hatch, Jack Townsend, and Captain Bill Rodney.
Courtesy of Mr. and Mrs. Earl Simpson

In 1936 Minnie Hearne Jones inherited the ownership of the Belmont Hotel. During this time she increased the room capacity and real estate holdings to absorb the Laurel Cottages on the oceanfront, renaming it the Hearne. She was married to Captain John B. Jones and was instrumental in the development of Ocean City.
Courtesy of Kathryn Jones Bunting

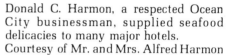

Donald C. Harmon, a respected Ocean City businessman, supplied seafood delicacies to many major hotels.
Courtesy of Mr. and Mrs. Alfred Harmon

Dr. Francis J. Townsend came from Snow Hill, Maryland, to Ocean City to practice medicine before the turn of the century. He arrived during the heyday of medicine wagons and itinerants dispensing patent medicines and giving medical advice along the streets of the town. During his lifetime Dr. Townsend untiringly served every medical need of the community. He married Anna Rayne of Ocean City and they had two children. Today his son, Francis, Jr., carries on the family tradition of medical care to the community.
Courtesy of
Dr. and Mrs. Francis J. Townsend, Jr.

The Washington Pharmacy, located at Somerset Street on the boardwalk, was owned by Dr. Francis J. Townsend, Sr. From this building he concocted many of his trusted prescriptions. The business no longer exists.

Courtesy of Mr. and
Mrs. Alan Quillin and family

Dr. Guy Dennis, Ocean City's first dentist.
Courtesy of Thelma Dennis and family

Ethel Griffin Kelley owned and operated two of the resort's larger hotels, the Royalton and the Beach Plaza, with her son Harry Kelley, Jr. The kitchens of her hotels were unsurpassed, and her generous hospitality drew many famous patrons through the years.
Courtesy of Harry Kelley, Jr.

117

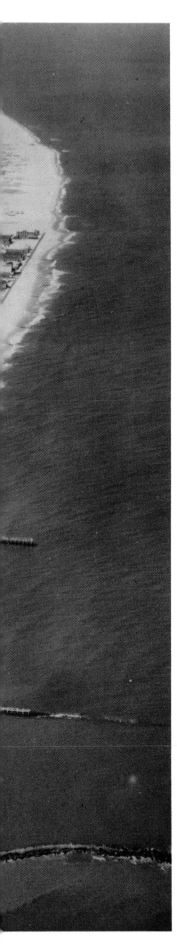

This exceptional aerial view of the town was taken September 23, 1936.
Courtesy of Eastern Shore Times, Inc.

Vacationers line the boardwalk in 1936 to admire contestants in the annual beauty parade.
Courtesy of Elizabeth Gordy for the Showell family

Grocery stores displaying their wares on the sidewalks have become a nicety of the past.
Courtesy of Mr. and Mrs. Alfred Harmon

The Sand Bar Casino was a popular gambling and night club attraction located on Thirty-Third Street. The building no longer exists.
Courtesy of Doris Dennis

Dr. Louis S. and Ruth Parsons were avid
sportfishing enthusiasts during the 1930s
and 1940s. A prominent surgeon from
Wilmington, Delaware, "Doc" Parsons
was highly respected in the community.
Courtesy of D. Frank Parsons
and Ocean City Museum Society

Mayor William Thomas Elliott and his wife Edna were photographed on the porch of their home in 1938. Elliott served as mayor during the years 1934 to 1938. He went to work at the fish camps as a young boy, and in 1916 he started his own fishing company. With his brother Joe, Elliott ran this business until the mid–forties. He was influential in many civic groups.

Courtesy of Mr. and Mrs. Charles Elliott

Captain Earl Powell, *left*, poses with his party of sport fishermen. This white marlin was taken aboard the *Duchess* in the summer of 1937.

Courtesy of Mr. and Mrs. Roland E. Powell

The first marlin of 1939 was caught by S. Dodd Shuster, aboard the cruiser *Dod-Jim II.* Pictured here are, *left to right,* Captain George Taylor, Dodd Shuster, Pearl Shuster, and Herbert Redden. During that year 1,259 marlin were caught off Ocean City.

Courtesy of Mr. and Mrs. Earl Simpson

Although not a common occurrence, through the years whales have beached themselves at Ocean City. After attempts to remove the whale with tow trucks failed, dynamite was used to blow the whale to pieces so that it would be easier to haul away. Unfortunately, every roof top in Ocean City caught the fallout and the town smelled of rotten fish for the next year.

Courtesy of Louis Chambliss

Elzie Ayres, a respected figure in Ocean City's business community. Ayres supplied ice and coal to the hotels and boardwalk concessions.
Courtesy of Mr. and Mrs. W. Preston Laws

Jester's Fun House as it appeared in 1941. The fun house was located on Worcester Street just off the Boardwalk. Laughing Sal, the larger-than-life laughing doll was the main attraction to thousands of boardwalk goers for over fifty years.

Courtesy of Irma J. Jester

This rare photograph taken in 1938 shows Ocean City's commercial harbor in its infancy. After the 1933 storm, two of the original fishing companies which had been located on the surf side merged to form the Davis and Lynch Fish Company. Located on the mainland directly behind today's inlet, this harbor was to become one of Ocean City's most valued commercial assets.

Courtesy of Ellen Lynch Weaver

Edmond H. Johnson served as mayor of
Ocean City from 1938 to 1940. A prominent lawyer of his day, he served as
state's attorney for Worcester County
1923-26, city solicitor of Ocean City, and
as attorney for the commissioners of this
county. In 1943 he was appointed asso-
ciate judge of the First Judicial Circuit.
Judge Johnson made Ocean City his home
during the greater part of his life.
    Courtesy of Alexandria Perdue

The Breakers Hotel, located on the
boardwalk at Third Street.
        Courtesy of Mr. and
    Mrs. Alan Quillin and family

The Dennis Hotel, shown here in 1938, was built near the turn of the century on the corner of Dorchester Street and Baltimore Avenue. The business was operated by the Dennis family until the 1960s, when the city government purchased the land for municipal parking.
Courtesy of Thelma Dennis and family

The Commander Hotel, located on the boardwalk at Fourteenth Street.
Courtesy of Mr. and
Mrs. Alan Quillin and family

Members of the Game Fisherman's Association journeyed to Washington to present President Roosevelt the first marlin caught during the 1938 season by Dodd Shuster of Wilmington, Delaware. Those who made the presentation to the President were: *left to right:* Talbot E. Bunting, John B. Lynch, W. Preston Laws, James D. Jarmon, and Captain Crawford Savage. An invitation to fish at Ocean City was extended, and in 1939 Roosevelt did fish off Ocean City from the Presidential yacht *Potomac;* he caught two marlin.

Courtesy of Mr. and
Mrs. W. Preston Laws

The Game Fish Association was the parent organization of today's Ocean City Marlin Club. D. Frank Parsons, pictured here, and Talbot Bunting represented this group in an early 1939 promotional effort at Philadelphia, Pennsylvania.
Courtesy of Ocean City Museum Society

Captain Talbot Bunting, son of Charles R. Bunting, Sr., a pioneer in Ocean City's early fishing industry, hoists a billfish onto the family dock located on Talbot Street.

Courtesy of Hilda Savage
for the Rounds family

The Norwegian freighter *Olaf Bergh* ran aground in 1941 during World War II. It was not uncommon for ships to hug the coastline to avoid being targets for German submarines. The captain of this vessel reportedly mistook the Fenwick Lighthouse for the entrance to the Delaware Bay and came ashore at Ninety-Fourth Street. Several weeks later the *Olaf Bergh* was floated off.

Courtesy of Melville Quillin

Tappen Phillips and James Farlow, members of the Ocean City Coast Guard, guide a crewman of the *Olaf Bergh* to safety by means of a breeches buoy.

Courtesy of
Mr. and Mrs. William Bunting

The Ocean City marlin fleet inaugurates the 1940 fishing season. Four thousand spectators jammed the boardwalk and jetty as the boats passed in review through the inlet to the Atlantic Ocean. Assateague Island and the south jetty, shown in the background, have changed drastically in the thirty-nine years since this photograph was taken.

Courtesy of Mrs. Joshua Bunting
and family

For many years residents had to travel to Berlin, seven miles inland, to bank at either of that town's two banking companies, or use a much-practiced form of mattress banking. Levin D. Lynch, pictured here with his wife, Betty, was instrumental in forming Ocean City's first bank, The Bank of Ocean City, in 1916. He served as its president from 1916 to 1965.

Courtesy of Mrs. Joshua Bunting and family

The Ocean City Volunteer Fire Company poses during the 1940s.

Courtesy of Ocean City Volunteer Fire Company

Mayor Clifford P. Cropper served as chief executive for the city from 1940 to 1944. Cropper owned and operated one of the many fish camps during the early era of pound fishing. He continued with the business after the 1933 storm and was one of the first to introduce trawlers into the commercial fishing business. Cropper played an influential role in the growth of the Presbyterian Church.

Courtesy of Etta Cropper Davidson

Captains Joe and Tom Elliott are pictured on the loading platform of the company was one of three of the original fish companies to continue with pound fishing after the 1933 storm.

Courtesy of Mr. and Mrs. Charles Elliott

Bathing beauties of the late 1940s. Local girls pose for this promotional photograph in the surf at Ocean City. *Left to right:* Lillian Taylor Townsend, Esther Simpson Rayne, Imogene Taylor Pierce, Hannah Ayres Esham.

Courtesy of Frank Townsend, Jr.

A boardwalk scene during the 1940s.
Courtesy of Mr. and Mrs. Alfred Harmon

Construction of a new access bridge was completed in 1944 between Caroline and North Division streets.

Courtesy of Elizabeth Gordy for the Showell family

The crew of the Ocean City Coast Guard Station at Ocean City, during the 1940s. *Left to right, standing:* Levin Bunting, Jr., Jack Pusey, William Burbage, Charles Adyolette, William Parker, Claude Donnaway; *seated:* William Massey, Wilmer Cropper, Thomas Moore, Harry D. Mitchell, James Farlow.

Courtesy of Mr. and Mrs. William Burbage

The Ocean City Beach Patrol during the 1940s. *Right to left, standing*: Howard Shipley, Ernest Travis, Robert Craig, John Neunnan, unidentified, unidentified; *seated*: unidentified, Toby Fields, John D. Showell III, James Parker, Earl Simpson, George Lynch, unidentified; *kneeling*: Thomas Price.

Courtesy of Elizabeth Gordy for the Showell family

Colored Day at Ocean City in the 1940s. Until the mid-1950s, during the week following Labor Day, two days were set aside for blacks to enjoy the beach and boardwalk. Henry's Colored Hotel was the only establishment on the island where transit workers could stay, but head chefs and waiters were given small basement rooms in most of the larger hotels. As in many Southern coastal communities, only a select few blacks were allowed to live on the island proper. John D. Showell, Sr., and his granddaughter Margaret Strohecker are *center, left* in the photograph.

Courtesy of Margaret Hall for the Showell family

The Lankford Hotel, Eighth Street and
the boardwalk.
Courtesy of
Mr. and Mrs. Alfred Harmon

This Douglas Devastater divebomber
crashed on the beach just north of the
pier during the early years of World
War II. The plane was on a submarine
patrol along the coast. The aircraft was
repaired, then pulled onto Route 50,
which the pilot used as a runway and
took off.
Courtesy of Gennette McCabe

The Mayflower Hotel, Twelfth Street and
the boardwalk.
Courtesy of
Mr. and Mrs. Alfred Harmon

The George Washington Hotel, Tenth
Street and the boardwalk.
Courtesy of
Mr. and Mrs. Alfred Harmon

139

Left to right: Governor Herbert O'Connor, Minnie Massey, Ella Dennis, and Mayor Daniel Trimper, Jr., in 1945, Mrs. Massey was honored as Ocean City's oldest resident, and Mrs. Dennis as the oldest continuous hotel operator.
Courtesy of Thelma Dennis and family

Earl and Imogene Pierce perform a song-and-dance routine during the 1940s. This form of fund raising for Ocean City's non-profit organizations absorbed many entertaining evenings during the winter months.
Courtesy of Thelma Dennis and family

Men stationed at the Ocean City Coast Guard Station are pictured showing off in 1946. Wearing the out-of-date, Showell rental bathing suits are *left to right:* Corky, Roland "Fish" Powell who would one day become the mayor of Ocean City, Charles Calhoun, "Tiny" Pruitt, and William "Bill" Parker.
Courtesy of Susan Powell Wenzlaff

A souvenir found in an old scrapbook is a fond remembrance to those who attended the Pier Club when it was at its pinnacle. The building today houses Ripley's Believe It Or Not Museum.
Courtesy of
Mrs. Joshua Bunting and family

Reliving World War II experiences were, *left to right:* Frank Massey, William Burbage, Harold Rayne, Jr., Turner Cropper, Jr., and Harry Bunting, Jr. This photograph was taken during a celebration party held for returning veterans at the Pier Ballroom.
Courtesy of
Mr. and Mrs. Turner Cropper, Jr.

It's Smart To Be Seen at The
P ★ I ★ E ★ R   C ★ L ★ U ★ B

OCEAN CITY ★ MARYLAND

During the summer of 1949, Joshua Bunting and Reese Layton, *right*, are shown with the first sharks caught in Sinepuxent Bay for sport.
Courtesy of Mrs. Joshua Bunting and family

"Planting the first umbrella of 1946" was a post-World War II promotional photograph for Ocean City. *Left to right:* Suzanne Mason, Mary Lou Mason, Mayor Daniel Trimper, Governor Herbert O'Connor, Betsy Jane Dennis, and Esther Simpson. Trimper served the community as mayor from 1944 to 1959. Through his promotional efforts Ocean City's tourist industry experienced steady growth.
Courtesy of Thelma Dennis and family

In 1946 the citizens of Ocean City celebrated the return of its men from World War II. *Left to right:* Ethel Esham, Evelyn Quillin, Robert Quillin, Louise Duer, Joshua Bunting, and Lester Esham at the Pier Ballroom.
Courtesy of Mrs. Joshua Bunting and family

The Sandy Hill cottages, the small cluster of buildings in the near center of this photograph, were the beginning of what is now known as motel row. This aerial view, taken in the late 1940s, shows the area encompassing Fifteenth to Thirtieth Streets.
  Courtesy of Ocean City Public Relations

This interior view of W. P. Laws' store was taken in 1948. Mr. and Mrs. Laws started this business in 1919. The establishment supplied groceries for most of the hotels and rooming houses in the town. Mr. Laws holds the official titles of Mr.. Easter and Mr. Ocean City, and was instrumental in the forming of Ocean City's Chamber of Commerce. Mrs. Laws was a teacher in the community for many years.

Courtesy of Mr. and Mrs. W. Preston Laws

A late 1940s aerial view of the Ship Cafe Restaurant and Marina also shows the Rick's Raft Club near the top of the photograph. The area was sparsely populated until the mid-1960s.

Courtesy of Ocean City Public Relations

The old Catholic Home was remodeled to The LaGrande Hotel in 1948. The building was one of the first to be built on the island. Built at Thirteenth Street the building was considered "way out of town" during the 1940s and early 1950s. Bob Ching, had his well-remembered restaurant in the basement of the hotel.

Courtesy of Maude Gaskins

The Commander Hotel, located on Fourteenth Street, was in 1946 considered by locals to be "up the beach" at the extreme north end of town. The Catholic Home, to the immediate left of the hotel, formerly known as St. Rose's Summer Home for the Orphans, was built in 1898 and remained Ocean City's most northern building until the Commander was built in the early 1930s.

Courtesy of Ocean City Public Relations

Crowds gather to watch a prize catch being unboated at the Dorchester Street docks.
Courtesy of Mrs. Joshua Bunting and family

The Ocean City High School girls basketball team in 1951. *Left to right, kneeling:* Phyllis Tilghman, Shirley Ludlam, Joyce Savage, June Kitchens, and Sue Brittingham. *Left to right, second row:* Ann Payne, Maude Cropper, Marion Mumford, Mildred Ann Adkins, Joyce Jarmon, and Shirley Richardson. *Left to right, standing:* Pauline Willis, Marie Gulyas, Lola Hastings, Sarah Cropper, Patricia Hall, and Irma Hudson.
Courtesy of George and Suzanne Hurley

A July 4th Celebration was held in 1944 to honor returning war hero Lieutenant Robert Lee Cropper. The pilot of a torpedo plane, he distinguished himself by sending to the bottom, both a heavy and a light Japanese cruiser at Rabaul Harbor, New Britain. He also scored a hit with a two-thousand-pound bomb that sank a transport in the Indian Ocean. For this heroism and extraordinary achievement Cropper was the recipient of the Distinguished Service Cross as well as the Purple Heart which was presented to him by Admiral William F. Halsey, commander of the South Pacific area. Cropper is the son of Harry and Harriett Hickman Cropper.

The 1951 Ocean City High School Basketball Championship team. The entire male population of the high school was thirty. From 1949 until 1952 they won four county and Eastern Shore championships culminating in the state championship in 1952. *Left to right standing:* Manager George Jackson, John Russell, Robert Lewis, Steve Guyas, Burt Raliegh, George Hurley, Paul Brown, and Coach Charles Dondero. *Left to right kneeling:* William Brown, Forrest Bradford, Albert Willis, Lionel Massey, James Shockley, and Robert West.

Courtesy of
the Ocean City Museum Society

Fishing for dolphin in 1939, were left to right: bothers Bob and Charles Jackson, two sportsmen from the city and captain of the *Daisey-Lee*, Bill Burbage.

Courtesy of Sally Bunting

The first blue marlin was caught off Ocean City in 1941, the second the next day. Pictured here is the third blue marlin, which was not boated until 1953. Captain William Burbage, left, with angler Jim Booze, displays this 413-pound blue caught aboard the Cecil.

Courtesy of Mr. and Mrs. William Burbage

John Bergman continued into the late 1950s an old tradition of peddling fresh fish to hotels and rooming houses.

Courtesy of Allen Bergman

On December 30, 1958, the *African Queen* was bound from Colombia, South America, to Paulsboro, New Jersey, with two hundred thousand barrels of crude oil aboard when she met disaster. Seven miles due east of Ocean City the tanker ran aground on a "hump" covered by twenty-seven feet of water, and broke in two. Forty-seven crewmen were rescued by Coast Guard, Marine, and Navy helicopters, and were brought safely to Ocean City.
Courtesy of Ocean City Museum Society

Mayor Hugh Thomas Cropper, Jr., and his father Hugh, Sr., are pictured in the early 1950s at their gunning lodge on Assateague Island. Mayor Cropper served the community from 1959 until 1970. Under his leadership much of the groundwork for the phenomenal growth of Ocean City was laid; the annexation of Forty-Fifth Street to the Delaware line and the installation of water and sewerage line, encouraging growth in the northern section of the island, took place under this administration.

Courtesy of Mr. and
Mrs. Hugh T. Cropper, Jr.

John J. and Sarah Coffin Rayne, shown in a 1951 photograph, owned several businesses in the downtown area, one of which, J. J. Rayne and Son, a luncheonette, is still operated by the family.

Courtesy of Manna Rayne

David Lynch, left, and his father Levin D. Lynch are pictured here in this early 1950s promotional photograph of the clamming industry at Ocean City. The Lynch name was synonymous with commercial fishing at the resort.

Courtesy of Ellen Lynch Weaver

A raging surf pounds against the Sea Scape Motel as the storm of 1962 begins. Photograph by Owen Mumford; courtesy of Mr. and Mrs. J. D. Quillin III Collection

Beachfront property between Forty-Ninth and Fiftieth streets during and after the storm.
Courtesy of Mr. and Mrs. J. D. Quillin III Collection

155

Damage to the beachfront at Nineteenth
and Twentieth streets.
        Courtesy of Mr. and
Mrs. J. D. Quillin III Collection

Damage caused by the storm to buildings
along the oceanfront.
Courtesy of Mr. and
Mrs. J. D. Quillin III Collection

An aerial view of Ocean City taken
during the winter of 1962 shows Twenty-
Fifth Street looking north.
Courtesy of Mr. and
Mrs. J. D. Quillin III Collection

At Seventieth Street a new inlet was
formed, making evacuation from this
point north impossible during the height
of the storm. The one fatality of the storm
was the occupant of the car submerged in
this photograph.
Courtesy of Mr. and
Mrs. J. D. Quillin III Collection

The aftermath of the March 1962 storm between Thirty-Third and Thirty-Fifth streets.

Courtesy of Mr. and Mrs. J.D. Quillin III Collection

The Right Reverend Eugene T. Stout, a kind, gentle, and progressive man, served Saint Mary's Star of the Sea Catholic Church from 1940 to 1974.
Courtesy of Eastern Shore Times, Inc.

Former Maryland Governor Marvin Mandel, *left*, stands beside his first white marlin. Captain Reade Miles and mate Junior Truitt of the *Renie B* stand to the right of the governor's billfish. Mandel was in Ocean City in 1969 tuning up for the fifth annual Governor's Invitational White Marlin Tournament.
Courtesy of Ocean City Public Relations

The oldest continuously operated merry-go-round in the United States, located in the Windsor Resorts, has been the delight of many generations of Ocean City visitors.
Courtesy of Eastern Shore Times, Inc.

Actor Robert Mitchum, *right*, a visitor to Ocean City for many years, is pictured with Ship Cafe owner Pete Boinis and Mrs. John Chanell in 1971.
Photograph by John Mick; courtesy of Eastern Shore Times, Inc.

One of the famous Mason-Dixon boundary markers can be found near the base of the Fenwick Lighthouse located on the Maryland-Delaware line.
Courtesy of Eastern Shore Times, Inc.

United States Senator Barry Goldwater speaks at a convention held in Ocean City in 1973.
Courtesy of Eastern Shore Times, Inc.

Country and western singer Conway Twitty entertains crowds at the shore in 1974.
Courtesy of Eastern Shore Times, Inc.

Former Vice-President Spiro Agnew is a frequent guest and an Ocean City property owner.
Courtesy of Eastern Shore Times, Inc.

In Ocean City for a performance, Al Martino captivates night club crowds.
Courtesy of Eastern Shore Times, Inc.

Former President Richard M. Nixon tours Assateague Island with members of the Department of the Interior in 1972. As Vice-President, he and his family came to the resort on several occasions to vacation at the Beach Plaza Hotel.
Courtesy of Eastern Shore Times, Inc.

Steven Ford, son of former President Gerald Ford, was a long-time vacationer at the resort. This photograph was taken shortly after his father was named President of the United States.
Courtesy of Eastern Shore Times, Inc.

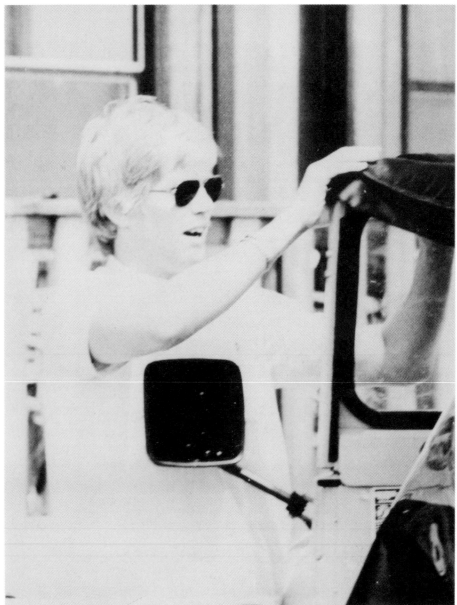

Promotional tours to large cities under the direction of Jim Gordon are sponsored by the mayor and city council each year. In 1969, at the Cleveland Show, Ocean City was also advertising for more doctors to locate in the area.
Courtesy of Ocean City Public Relations

Since 1968 convention groups from many states have enjoyed first class accommodations at Ocean City's Convention Hall. Many big name bands have performed here during the winter months. This aerial photograph was taken from the Atlantic surf looking westward, with the Isle of Wight Bay in the background.
Photograph by Robert J. Bennett; courtesy of Ocean City Public Relations

Perhaps the most dramatic transfigura-
tion that could occur to a town took place
in Ocean City during the early 1970s when
the so-called building boom was in
progress. This photograph shows the
construction of the Capri condominium.
Courtesy of Eastern Shore Times, Inc.

Ocean City's municipal airport was opera-
tional in 1956. Located on the mainland
just south of the resort, it today handles
seventy thousand operations per year. Due
to the prevailing winds and to better accommodate the increase in traffic, a new
north-south runway is presently being
constructed.
Courtesy of Ocean City Public Relations

The "Little Salisbury" section of Ocean City between 87th Street and 94th Street as it appeared in the mid 1970s.
Courtesy of Paul J. Smith

Huge steel derricks dotted the skyline of North Ocean City along High Rise Row during the height of the building boom that prefaced a new era for the city.
Courtesy of Eastern Shore Times, Inc.

North Ocean City at 96th Street as it appeared in 1962, before the building boom of the early 1970s.
Courtesy of James Burdette

Ocean City was a barren and desolate strip of beach on January 3, 1799, when Captain William Carhart of Philadelphia lost his life in a shipwreck. His is the only marked grave of a shipwrecked mariner in the area. The grave site is in Captain's Hill, so named for the man buried there.

Courtesy of James Gall

Due to the phenomenal growth which has transpired since 1965. Ocean City today has the appearance of a metropolitan city.

Courtesy of Eastern Shore Times, Inc.

A 1926 aerial view of the Glen Riddle Farm located three miles west of Ocean City. The 1,500-acre farm was once a center of American Thoroughbred racing. In addition to its fame, it was an integral part of the economy of this area as a major employer. The horses of Samuel D. Riddle were foaled in Lexington, Kentucky, and brought to this farm by railroad for training during the winter and spring. Man O' War sired an impressive line of champions that were trained here. His son, Battleship, was perhaps the most famous. In 1938 Battleship won the Grand National Steeplechase in England. The farm has recently been purchased from the Riddle heirs by an Arizona investor. It will be a planned housing development, golf course, and marina.

Courtesy of the Ocean City Museum Society

War Admiral—son of Man O' War—was the 1937 racing season champion. The winner of the Triple Crown in that year, he was trained at the Glen Riddle Farm three miles west of Ocean City. Shown here in 1938 with jockey M. Peters up at Saratoga, N.Y.
Courtesy of Billie Whaley Brittingham and William Whaley Brittingham

Samuel D. Riddle, left, and William Whaley, his manager at Saratoga, N.Y., in 1931. An Ocean City resident, Whaley managed the Glen Riddle Farm from 1925 to 1950.
Courtesy of Billie Whaley Brittingham and William Whaley Brittingham

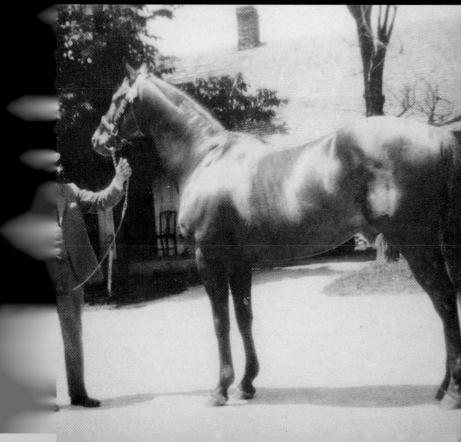

Man O' War was considered to be the greatest race hose ever bred in America. In the 1920s he shattered world and American time records. Described as "de mostest hoss dat ever was," he was trained on the Glen Riddle Farm three miles west of Ocean City. Samuel D. Riddle once refused an offer of a blank check for any amount for "Big Red," as the horse was nicknamed. He lived to the age of thirty and sired many champions. Shown here in retirement with manager William Whaley of Ocean City.
Courtesy of Billie Whaley Brittingham and William Whaley Brittingham

The aftermath of the 1962 storm (top—75th Street), and dredging projects of the late 1960s (bottom) made land readily available and reasonably priced entering the 1970s when the first building boom was experienced.

Courtesy of Mr. and Mrs. Roland E. Powell and Mr. Paul J. Smith

The Fenwick Lighthouse marks the northern boundary of Ocean City. Constructed in 1859 on what was then part of Assateague Island, it was built to help alleviate the many shipwrecks which were occurring on that barren stretch of beach due to the deceptive shoreline, severe storms, and disoriented sea captains. The lighthouse is located on the Maryland-Delaware line and stands eighty-three feet above water level; its light rays carry nineteen miles to sea. In December of 1978 it was deactivated by the United States Coast Guard after 119 years of service.

Courtesy of Dale Timmons

A 1978 aerial view of Montego Bay by Paul Smith. The mobile home park was developed in 1968 and today contains one thousand homes with a summer population of four thousand. The development extends from 130th to 134th streets on the west side of the island.

    Courtesy of Eastern Shore Times, Inc.

The wreck of the tug *Pauline Holmes* from which five men were rescued through the combined efforts of the Ocean City volunteer fire company and the Coast Guard during November 1977.

    Courtesy of Eastern Shore Times, Inc.

In 1977 one of Ocean City's first buildings was scheduled for demolition. Through the generosity of the mayor and city council, funds were made available to the newly formed Museum Committee to save this landmark. The building was moved in December 1977 from its location on Caroline Street down the beach to a new location on the boardwalk at the inlet. The building, renamed the Ocean City Life-Saving Station Museum, is scheduled to open during the summer of 1979.

Courtesy of
Mr. and Mrs. George M. Hurley

During the winter of 1978 Ocean City's beaches were severely damaged by a series of twenty-five northeast storms. A program was instigated to bulldoze sand from the ocean and use it as a buffer against erosion and the undermining of valuable beachfront property.

Courtesy of Ocean City Public Relations

William Parker, Sr., and Harry Dale Mitchell in 1929.
　　　Courtesy of William J. Massey family

Bathing fashions in 1910.
　　　Courtesy of Kathryn Jones Bunting

Ann Upshur Jarvis in 1932.
　　　Courtesy of Francis J. Townsend, Jr.

Presbyterian Church, 1978.
Courtesy of Larry Bright

Methodist Church, 1978.
Courtesy of Larry Bright

City Hall, 1978.
Courtesy of Larry Bright

Pony penning on Assateague in 1937. Large
herds of horses under private ownership,
these belonging to Elizabeth Powell, were
wintered on the island up until the time of
an attempted development by Louis
Ackerman in 1950.
 Courtesy of Mary Adeline Bradford

After the storm of 1933 and before the
building of the Verrazano Bridge in 1963,
the only way for vehicles to gain access to
Assateague Island was by way of the south
Point Ferry.
 Courtesy of William T. Byrd

How times have changed since John Dos Passos wrote of lodging at Ocean City in *The 42nd Parallel:* "In the dark hotel lobby lit by a couple of smoked oil lamps . . . up in the little pine bedroom . . . the roar of the surf came in through the rusty screen."

Photographs by Paul Smith
Courtesy of Eastern Shore Times, Inc.

The Quay

Antiqua

The Golden Sands

Blue Water East

Centruy I

The Atlantis

Pyramid

179

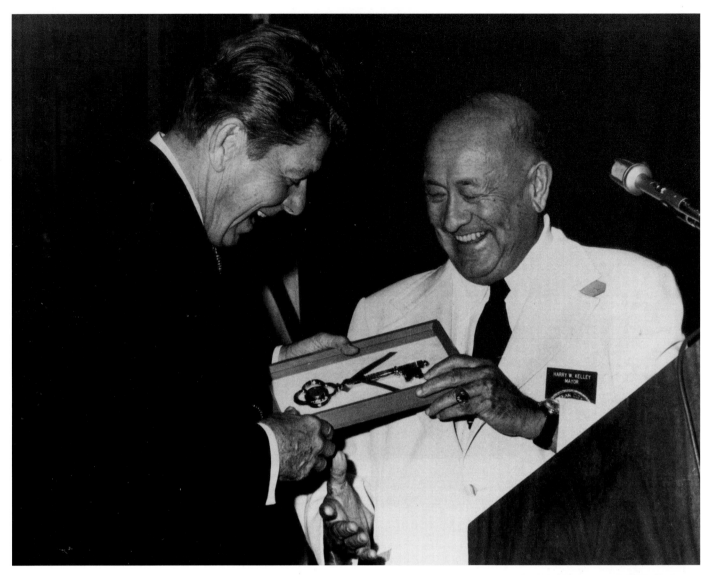

Harry Kelly, Mayor of Ocean City from 1970 to 1985 is shown here in 1984 presenting the Key to Ocean City, Maryland, to the President of the United States, Ronald Reagan.

Courtesy of Viola Thomas

Granville D. Trimper served as mayor of Ocean City following the untimely death of Mayor Kelley in 1985 until a special election could be held. He served as a city councilman for eighteen years, many of which were as president. During his tenure on the council the city experienced two unprecedented building booms following annexation to the Delaware line. He served until 1988.

Courtesy of the Town of Ocean City

Thelma C. Conner was the first woman elected to the Ocean City Council. The city manager form of government was adopted during her tenure. She was instrumental in establishing the Ocean City Life-Saving Station Museum and serves on the board of Wor-Wic Tech Community College. Mrs. Conner is the owner-operator of two Ocean City businesses; The Dunes Motel and the Dunes Manor Hotel.

Courtesy of Sandra Lee Hurley

Roland E. Powell is the present mayor of Ocean City. Born and raised in the area, he was first elected to the City Council in 1968 and served as council president during the early 1970s. Elected to the Worcester County Commissioners in 1974 he served in county government for twelve years, several as president of the commission. In 1985 he was elected as mayor of Ocean City. Perhaps the most significant accomplishment during his term of office to date has been the joint participation of the federal, state, county and city governments in the beach replenishment program.

Courtesy of the Town of Ocean City

"Wish You Were Here"

I DON'T CARE WHAT HAPPENS.
THAT'S HOW I FEEL.

at Ocean City, Md.

185

A Jolly Quartette, Ocean City, Md.

Two Queens and a Jack   At Ocean City, Md.   Alma

Greetings from
Ocean City, Md.

1-19-'07

I'M ENJOYING MYSELF HERE, BUT I'M NOT SHOWING MY FACE

Bibliography

Annual Report U. S. Life-Saving Service. Washington, D.C.: Department of the Treasury, Printed Archive Division, 1883.

Barth, John. *Lost in the Funhouse.* New York: Doubleday, 1969.

Dos Passos, John. *U.S.A.: The 42nd Parallel.* New York: Random House, 1937.

Malone, Lemuel. "Happenings." *Salisbury Advertiser,* 10 July 1875, Sec. 1, p. 3, col. 3.

Purnell, Charles W. "I Remember Ocean City 20 Years Ago Today." *Baltimore Sun Paper,* 23 Aug. 1953, Magazine section, p. 2, cols. 1-4.

Robbins, Geoffrey H. and Brian P. Henley. *The History of Ocean City, Maryland.* Ocean City, Md.: Ocean City Centennial Committee, 1975.

Truitt, Dr. Reginald V., and Dr. Millard G. Les Callette. *Worcester County: Maryland's Arcadia.* Baltimore: Waverly Press, 1977.

Tuoner, Frank, recording secretary. *Minutes of the Sinepuxent Beach Company of Baltimore City.* Ocean City, Md.: Atlantic Hotel Corp., section 1890-91.

White, S. K., and J. R. White. "Ocean City Pier Completed." *Salisbury Advertiser,* 6 July 1907, p. 1, col. 2.

Wroton, William H., Jr. *Assateague.* Cambridge, Md.: Tidewater Publishers, 1972.

Index